Who Really Wrote the Book of Mormon?

Who Really Wrote the Book of Mormon?

Howard A. Davis, Donald R. Scales & Wayne L. Cowdrey
with Gretchen Passantino

VISION HOUSE PUBLISHERS
Santa Ana, California 92705

DEDICATION

This book is dedicated to Walter Martin, author, comparative religion professor, and director of Christian Research Institute. He maintained for 25 years that Solomon Spalding was the true source of *The Book of Mormon*.

ACKNOWLEDGMENTS

We would like to thank all those whose help made our exhaustive research possible. Our deep appreciation is extended to Dr. Walter Martin and his assistant, Mr. Jerry Bodine, for their continued assistance in the project.

The excellent legal work of attorneys Reinjohn, Marchetti, and their associates supported this work a great deal. We would like to thank document experts Henry Silver, Howard Doulder, and William Kaye for their professional services.

David Hagelberg and Arthur Vanick labored on some of the most tedious portions of the manuscript, for which we are grateful. Kurt VanGorden obtained many valuable records and affidavits for us. Countless librarians supplied us with photostatic copies and microfilm materials which greatly aided our research. Mrs. Farabe, an instructor in Amity, Pennsylvania, and the wife of the great-great grandson of Joseph Miller (a close friend of Spalding), sent us a great amount of information on the Spalding issue. Gary Lloyd's information was also invaluable. We are grateful for the assistance of Mrs. M. C. Cowles of Oberlin College and of Oberlin's photographer, Stillwell, for supplying photographs and a microfilm of the Spalding manuscript.

A special note of thanks is due Terrie Broadaway, who led us to our first document expert. We are very thankful to all of our typists who worked so hard in this manuscript.

FOREWORD

I feel privileged to write the preface to a book whose impact will be, I am sure, almost incalculable. Since its beginning in 1820 (the year of its founder's first vision), the story of the Church of Jesus Christ of Latter Day Saints has been riddled wiih controversy. Opinion concerning the church's source ranged from those who said it was God's restoration of His true church, through suspicion of some sort of fraud, all the way to fiery denunciation of the supposed demonic entrapment of this "organization of Satan."

After extensive research into the "foundation stones" of the Mormon Church 25 years ago, I was convinced that I knew the true source of *The Book of Mormon,* one of the Latter Day Saints' sacred books. Although some agreed with me, most thought that my assertion of Spalding's part in the mystery of Mormonism was the assertion of one naive of the facts. For 25 years I have known that the Spalding source could be proved if one only had the time and the dedication to ferret it out. Wayne Cowdrey, Don Scales, and Howard Davis have had that dedication, and this book is the result.

Walter Martin, Ph.D.
Director, Christian Research Institute

CONTENTS

Introduction

In 1977 the Mormon Church (technically known as the Church of Jesus Christ of Latter Day Saints) claimed a worldwide membership of 3.1 million. Millions of people are trusting this church for their eternal destiny. They have been convinced that it is the *only* way to follow God's will. Zealous Mormons have for almost 150 years declared the Mormon Church to be the one true restoration of the church on earth today.

But the world must ask, can Mormonism back up its claims? Is it really the only way? Are its assertions true? Are blacks forever cursed, as this church teaches? Did Jesus really have many wives? Was He actually the spirit-brother of Lucifer, the offspring of Adam-God and Mary? Did Jesus really come to the Americas after His resurrection and preach the gospel to descendants of Jews who supposedly had peopled these continents?

The sacred books of the Mormons assert these doctrines and many more. Not content with the Bible as the only guide for faith and truth, the Mormon founders added to it three other books that are held by the church to be on a level higher than that of the Bible (which the Mormon Church claims is God's Word "in so far as it is correctly translated"). The other three books, *The Book of Mormon*, *The Pearl of Great Price*, and *Doctrine and Covenants*, contain the basis for all the teachings of the LDS Church. Each is supposed to be an infallible record of God's will for man, displayed in sacred history and utterances from on high both directly and through "prophets."

The Founder of Mormonism

The founder of Mormonism, Joseph Smith, Jr., claimed that in a grove near Palmyra, New York, in the spring of 1820, God the Father and God the Son appeared to him to answer his prayer about which religion was correct. The fifteen-year-old is said to have heard them tell him that ". . . they were all wrong, and the personage who addressed me said that all their creeds were an abomination in his sight; that those professors were all corrupt. . . ." The young visionary patiently waited for further communication from God, and was rewarded on September 21, 1823, when an angel appeared to him and told him of some fabulous "plates" which would reveal to him God's plans and dealings with America. The angel, named Moroni, said that the writings were on golden plates buried under a hill called Cumorah (near Joseph's home). At the proper time Joseph Smith was to dig up the plates and learn the history of the Americas.

Smith said that he went to this hill each year, waiting for instructions from God, until September 22, 1827, when he was finally commanded to dig up the plates. He used a lever to move a flat stone, and there in a stone box, according to Joseph Smith, his eyes beheld for the first time the golden plates, with a "breastplate" and two stones "set in silver bows," called the "Urim and Thummim." It was with the Urim and Thummim—and, according to Mormon sources, "the gift and power of God"—that Smith laboriously and meticulously

---

aSuch a type of Egyptian is nonexistent, according to Egyptologists.

translated the mysterious symbols (he called them "reformed Egyptian")[a] on the golden plates. His translation was said to be dictated to his friend, Oliver Cowdery,[b] and other scribes between 1828 and 1829. This 275,000-word document is known today throughout the world as the first of the Mormon sacred books, *The Book of Mormon*. Each volume today is prefaced by the testimony of eight men who each claimed that they had seen Smith's golden plates. Three other signatures offer testimony that the men saw the plates and viewed and heard an angel of God assuring them of the truth of the book.

Contested Origins

Serious scholars have long contested this story of the origin of *The Book of Mormon*. From the first public circulation of Smith's story, controversy has raged as to the true source of the stories of America's past. It is scarcely possible to find an informed non-Mormon who puts any credence in the "official" story, and yet these non-Mormon critics differ among themselves as to the true story.

Basically, two theses are the most widely held. The first school of thought believes that Joseph Smith, Jr., was the author of *The Book of Mormon*, and that the entire production was one of his own imagination. Various ideas have circulated as to whether he took any other people into his confidence and enlisted their aid. (Some say only Oliver Cowdery, others say one or more of the scribes besides Cowdery, and still others say it was someone not otherwise associated with Mormonism.)

---

[b]Oliver's last name was spelled Cowdery, while many of his descendants today spell their last name Cowdrey, as does one of the coauthors of this book.

The second major thesis teaches that Joseph Smith used a manuscript previously in existence. The assertion is that a retired Congregationalist minister, Solomon Spalding[c] (1761-1816), wrote a biblically styled novel called *The Manuscript Found*. A young man named Sidney Rigdon either took or copied this manuscript as it lay in a printing office in Pittsburgh, Pennsylvania. Rigdon and Cowdery (a cousin of Smith) remodeled the Spalding manuscript and presented it to the world not as a novel but as a divinely inspired record called *The Book of Mormon*.

If Joseph Smith actually used another man's novel and deceived millions of people into believing that God was speaking through this book, or if he deliberately invented a religion which is no religion at all, but instead a hoax of monstrous proportions, then millions of innocent people have been misled. Keep in mind that 10 percent of every obedient Mormon's income is given to his church unhesitatingly, because he is confident that he is giving to God.

The Book of Abraham

Careful scholarship has already proved that Joseph Smith was wrong about *The Pearl of Great Price*, the second of the Mormon sacred books. In 1967 the Metropolitan Museum of Art in New York City gave a collection of papyrus manuscripts to the Mormon Church in Salt Lake City. These were identified by the Mormons as the long-lost *Book of Abraham*, part of *The Pearl of Great Price*. Confident of the vindication which Joseph Smith and Mormonism would receive from the

---

[c]Solomon and his immediate family spelled their name Spalding, while other relatives, acquaintances, and descendants spelled it Spaulding.

translation of these pieces, the task of translation was promptly assigned to Dee Jay Nelson, a recognized Egyptologist and at the time, a Mormon.

Nelson found that the famous *Book of Abraham* was not a sacred history from God at all, but came from the Egyptian *Book of Breathings*, one of several religious prayers and writings traditionally placed in the tombs of the Egyptian dead centuries before Christ. Because of his discovery and the Mormon Church's refusal to acknowledge his facts, Nelson resigned from the Mormon Church with his wife and daughter and now publicly denounces Joseph Smith's *Book of Abraham*. (See Appendix 1 for Professor Nelson's verbatim statements of his findings.)

The other sacred Mormon book, *Doctrine and Covenants*, has also lost its claim to divine infallibility which it once held. Although calling it Scripture, the LDS Church has through the years yielded to other influences and changed its position on some of the teachings contained in this book. For example, although polygamy was purportedly revealed by God to Joseph as an "everlasting covenant" (see *Doctrine and Covenants* 132:1-4), Mormon president Wilford Woodruff was apparently convinced by the government to state in 1890, "We are not teaching polygamy or plural marriage, nor permitting any person to enter into its practice . . ." (*Doctrine and Covenants*, pp. 256-57). With the demise of the authority of the Bible (the continuing Mormon contention being that it is at least partly incorrectly translated) along with the diminishing authority of *The Pearl of Great Price* and *Doctrine and Covenants*, *The Book of Mormon* is thereby the only unassailed bulwark of LDS infallibility that remains. If the authority of *The Book of Mormon* is disproved, the last vestige of Mormon extrabiblical authority is nullified.

After hundreds of hours of painstaking research, we have come to a firm and studied conviction: *The Book of Mormon* is not a genuine revelation from God at all, but was derived from a novel written by Solomon Spalding. In this book we shall present the overwhelming evidences that convinced us that Solomon Spalding is actually the source of the composition now known as *The Book of Mormon*, originally a novel titled *The Manuscript Found*. We ask only that you read this book carefully and come to your own reasoned conclusion as to the true source of *The Book of Mormon*.

Wayne L. Cowdrey
Donald R. Scales
Howard A. Davis
November, 1977

The Roots
of Mormonism

Mormonism today claims 3.1 million members and boasts that every day, somewhere in the world, a new chapel is being dedicated. Mormons have risen to powerful financial and political heights throughout most of America. The country's largest bank has prominent stockholders who are Mormons, and Mormons wield powerful influence on far-ranging corporate interests. Associated Press writers Bill Beecham and David Brisco have stated that the Mormon Church's income exceeds one billion dollars yearly. The same article referred to a statement by former Salt Lake City mayor Lee that in 1962 the Mormon Church took in a million dollars per day.[1]

How did such a monumental enterprise originate? What is the reason for the devotion of the Mormon people to such an edifice? These questions are concerned with the history of Mormonism and with the lives of its founders and early leaders. Once we have a brief background of the Mormon story, some of its peculiar doctrines will be readily understandable.

One problem with Mormon history, however, is that the story as told by the Mormon Church is vastly different from that told by non-Mormons, both then and now. It is our contention that the true story has never been told by the Mormon Church, and we will present solid evidence showing that Mormonism's roots are not what Mormonism claims. Even a quick survey of the objective views of the history of Mormonism, stated by the people who were there at the time, shows discrepancies that no honest person could tolerate. First we will look at the history of Mormonism from a Mormon's point of view, and then we will devote the rest of our book to what actually happened based on reliable evidence gathered with painstaking care.

Joseph Smith

December 23, 1805, was the birthdate of Joseph Smith, Jr. He was born in Vermont, the third son of Joseph and Lucy Smith. When Joseph, Jr., was eleven years old his family located near Palmyra, New York. It was here that Mormonism was born. Although most of the Smith family joined the Presbyterian church, Joseph, Jr., stated that he was concerned about the divisions among denominations, and so decided to ask God for answers in accordance with James 1:5 ("If any of you lack wisdom, let him ask of God, that giveth to all men liberally, and upbraideth not, and it shall be given him"). Smith gives this account of what happened on a

spring day in 1820 when he went to the woods to pray as
a seeking fifteen-year-old.

> Owing to the many reports which have been put in cir-
> culation by evil-disposed and designing persons, in
> relation to the rise and progress of the Church of Jesus
> Christ of Latter-Day Saints, all of which have been
> designed by the authors thereof to militate against its
> character as a Church and its progress in the world—I
> have been induced to write this history, to disabuse
> the public mind, and put all inquirers after truth in
> possession of the facts, as they have transpired, in
> relation both to myself and the Church, so far as I have
> such facts in my possession. . . . I saw a pillar of light
> exactly over my head, above the brightness of the sun,
> which descended gradually until it fell upon me. . . .
> When the light rested upon me I saw two Personages,
> whose brightness and glory defy all description,
> standing above me in the air. One of them spake unto
> me, calling me by name, and said, pointing to the
> other—"This is My Beloved Son. Hear Him!". . . . I
> asked the Personages who stood above me in the light,
> which of all the sects was right—and which I should
> join.
>   I was answered that I must join none of them for
> they were all wrong; and the Personage who addressed
> me said . . . "they draw near to me with their lips, but
> their hearts are far from me; they teach for doctrines
> the commandments of men, having a form of
> godliness, but they deny the power thereof."
>   He again forbade me to join with any of them;
> and many other things did he say unto me, which I
> cannot write at this time.[2]

This is known in Mormon church history as Joseph
Smith's first vision. It was at this time, according to
Smith, that he learned that all religions were wrong.

Three years later, on September 21, 1823, Smith had
his second vision. In this vision the angel Moroni
appeared at Smith's bedside and purportedly told him

that God was calling him to a great work. In Smith's words:

> He called me by name, and said unto me that he was a messenger sent from the presence of God to me, and that his name was Moroni; that God had a work for me to do; and that my name should be had for good and evil among all nations, kindreds, and tongues, or that it should be both good and evil spoken of among all people.
>
> He said there was a book deposited, written upon gold plates, giving an account of the former inhabitants of this continent, and the source from whence they sprang. He also said that the fullness of the everlasting Gospel was contained in it, as delivered by the Savior to the ancient inhabitants;
>
> Also, that there were two stones in silver bows— and these stones, fastened to a breastplate, constituted what is called the Urim and Thummim—deposited with the plates; and the possession and use of these stones were what constituted "seers" in ancient or former times; and that God had prepared them for the purpose of translating the book. . . .
>
> Again, he told me, that when I got those plates of which he had spoken—for the time that they should be obtained was not yet fulfilled—I should not show them to any person; neither the breastplate with the Urim and Thummim; only to those to whom I should be commanded to show them; if I did I should be destroyed. . . .[3]

It was on the next day that Smith said he went to a hill outside the town (called the hill Cumorah) and found the golden plates in a stone box along with the breastplate, the Urim and the Thummim. However, the angel appeared again, according to Smith, and would not allow him to take the contents of the box. It was not until September 22, 1827, that Smith was permitted to take the things in the box, and it was not until 1830 that his "translation" was completed, with the aid of Oliver

Cowdery, a former schoolteacher. This "translation" of the golden plates was published in 1830 and was first sold on March 26 at the Palmyra bookstore. It is essentially what we know today as *The Book of Mormon*.

Joseph Smith told the story that Oliver Cowdery, Martin Harris (who financed the first printing), and David Whitmer saw the golden plates in a vision in which an angel appeared holding the plates and turning the pages. Eight other people were eventually permitted to see the plates by the angel, and the witness of these eleven men is still found at the beginning of every authentic copy of *The Book of Mormon. Be sure to notice that none of these men* (except Joseph) *ever saw the plates except in a vision.* No one except Smith ever claimed to have handled these plates, and no concrete evidence was ever brought forward to prove that they actually existed.

Mormon Beginnings

The Church of Jesus Christ of Latter Day Saints was officially organized on April 6, 1830, and was incorporated later that year. There were only six members at its inception, but that number had grown to forty after only one month.

At this time one of the distinctive Mormon doctrines was already clearly in evidence. In addition to rejection of all other denominations, Mormonism is adamant concerning the vital importance of its priesthoods. The Mormon Church maintains that there are two priesthoods, the Aaronic and the Melchisedec, that must be practiced today, and that these are attainable only through a practice called "the laying on of hands" by one who is designated by God. The original conferring of the priesthoods in the Mormon Church was allegedly performed by none other than John the Baptist (the Aaronic priesthood) and Peter, James, and John (the Melchisedec priesthood) on Smith and Cowdery in 1829. Subsequent ordinations to the priesthood were less ostentatious and glamorous, being performed by ordinary men in the church who had attained the position deemed necessary for conferring the priesthoods.

Since much of *The Book of Mormon* is concerned with the American Indians, Joseph decreed that an intense missionary activity be started at once among the Indians. Ostensibly for this purpose a number of Mormons, the first missionaries, went to Kirtland, Ohio, to evangelize the Indians. There in November 1830 Sidney Rigdon was baptized in the Mormon Church. Supposedly this evangelistic effort by the missionaries was Rigdon's first exposure to Mormonism and Joseph Smith. We will present evidence later in this book to show that this was not the case at all, and that in fact Rigdon knew about Mormonism before Joseph Smith ever claimed his first revelations!

According to early Mormon revelations (*Doctrine and Covenants* 57:1,2), Independence, Missouri, was to be the new Zion, in fulfillment of prophecy. The church moved there, but under persecution soon moved to Far West, Missouri. Finally the church relocated to Illinois, naming their new community Nauvoo.

Nauvoo became somewhat like an independent little country, with Joseph Smith, Jr., being the commander-in-chief of its army. Here at Nauvoo another temple was built for the Mormons' unique worship services.

However, an anti-Mormon newspaper, the *Nauvoo Expositor*, began raising the ire of Joseph Smith by printing what the Mormons asserted were lies and fabrications about the church and its leader. According to the Mormons, Joseph and his brother Hyrum were unfairly arrested and jailed in Carthage, Illinois, not far from Nauvoo. On June 27, 1884, Joseph and Hyrum Smith were both killed by a jail-storming crowd.

Brigham Young

Immediately upon the death of Joseph Smith, Jr., several contenders for the Mormon throne claimed the right to rule the now-numerous members of the Mormon Church. The three most important contenders were Joseph's son (represented by his mother and others, since he was a minor at the time), Sidney Rigdon (who was at that time the first counselor to Joseph Smith and who, we will show, may actually have had the right to take over, since we believe he was the originator of the Mormon religion), and Brigham Young (who was the president of the Mormon governing body called The Twelve Apostles).

Young was duly elected by the governing officers of the church (amid much dissension by the supporters of the other two contenders), and the majority of the Mormons followed his leadership unquestioningly. Those who refused to accept Young's appointment lost their membership in his church, and thus arose some of the many sects or divisions of Mormonism, the strongest of which is still active today and known as the Reorganized Church, under the direction of Joseph Smith's direct descendants. (Its first president was Joseph's son as soon as he reached adulthood.)

Brigham Young (1801-77) was a strong-willed man who saw for his church a vision far grander than anyone had hoped for before. In his plans was a virtually autonomous state or country under the leadership of himself as God's anointed one. With this vision and an eviction notice from the state of Illinois, Brigham and his followers left Nauvoo for the West in early February of 1846.

The hardships which the caravan encountered on the way have been well chronicled in movies and stories and need not be detailed here. As a credit to those Mormons who made the trip, it was an exodus of bravery and stalwartness that gave inspiration to later travelers through the rigorous terrain of the largely unexplored western United States.

On July 24, 1847, Brigham Young stopped the caravan in Salt Lake Valley, Utah. Shortly after that, he founded Salt Lake City, just ten miles from the shores of the Great Salt Lake. From that time to this, the city has been the headquarters of the Church of Jesus Christ of Latter Day Saints; faithful Mormons migrate to it today just as they did in the early years of its growth. From its meager beginnings in 1830 with six members, the Mormon Church has grown to astronomical proportions today.

The Church Today

The organization of today's Mormon Church is much the same as that originally conceived by Joseph Smith and developed by Brigham Young. The smallest operating unit within the church is the mission: there are about one hundred active missions around the world. There are twenty times as many mission *branches*, which together with the missions coordinate and execute the evangelical outreaches of the church proper. Within the church system are independent branches, wards, and stakes, which correspond roughly to what many churchgoers would think of as fledgling congregations, congregrations, and regional associations or conferences. The Mormon Church currently boasts well over three million adherents among these different groupings.

There are Mormons in almost every country in the world and in every state in the United States. The greatest number of Mormons live in Utah, but there are also large Mormon populations in Hawaii, California, and Arizona.[4]

There are sixteen temples in which the elaborate Mormon ceremonies are held, and these are located in Utah, Arizona, Idaho, California, Hawaii, Washington, D.C., New Zealand, Switzerland, and England. The elaborate temple ceremonies include celestial marriage and baptism for the dead.

The celestial marriage ceremony has been performed in its present ritual since President Wilford Woodruff purportedly received a revelation to the effect that polygamy (called by Joseph an everlasting ordinance in *Doctrine and Covenants* 132:1-4) was not to be physical and earthly, but should be confined to the future state of the faithful Mormon males, elevated after death to godhood. A woman "sealed" to a Mormon male in celestial marriage can look forward to a future life as a goddess.

The Mormons also believe that any descendant can be baptized as a stand-in for a dead relative if that descendant is a Mormon. (This is known as the Mormon doctrine of baptism for the dead.) The dead ancestor then has a greater chance to progress through the Mormon stages of heaven.

Another Mormon dogma concerns the two priesthoods administered by the church. Any Mormon white male may become a member of the Aaronic priesthood after the age of twelve so long as he understands the teachings of the church and is faithful to perform all the duties assigned him by the church. Those who desire to belong to the greater priesthood, the

Melchisedec, must wait until they are at least nineteen. All the members of the ruling bodies of the Mormon Church are and must be members of the Melchisedec priesthood.

The governing bodies of the church are the presidency and the Council of Twelve Apostles. The presidency is composed of the President and his two counselors. The Council of Twelve, though usually in a lesser position of power, rules in the event of the death of the President and votes a new President into power.

Two other well-known features of today's Mormon Church are its missionary program and its tithing. Most young Mormon men devote two years of their lives to bringing the gospel of Mormonism to people all over the world. Rarely, women or couples join the mission field. While missionaries, the young men must rely on family and friends for all of their support, as none comes from the church, and they are not permitted to be employed during their missionary stint.

Tithing 10 percent of one's income is mandatory if one desires to be an obedient member of the Mormon Church. In addition, donations are often solicited for other funds not covered by the tithes, and faithful Mormons are encouraged to maintain a year's supply of food.

Mormonism is today one of the fastest-growing religious bodies in the United States. Its adherents are loyal and absolutely committed to the teachings of the church's founder, Joseph Smith, Jr. Through his *Book of Mormon* and his other writings, Smith's gospel has been spread throughout the world. If the origin of *The Book of Mormon* is other than heavenly, then 3.1 million people today have been deceived by a fraudulent document.

NOTES

1. Bill Beecham and David Brisco, *Honolulu Advertiser,* Oct. 2, 1975.
2. LeGrand Richards, *A Marvelous Work and a Wonder* (Deseret Book Company, 1968), pp. 9-10.
3. Ibid., pp. 43-44.
4. The Reorganized Church is concentrated in Missouri, although it has branches in most metropolitan areas.

The Sacred Books of Mormonism

There are three bastions of Mormon authority and inspiration: *The Book of Mormon, The Pearl of Great Price,* and *Doctrine and Covenants.* The Bible, although revered as God's Word by Mormons, occupies a much lower position of authority than do these three books, since Mormons have been told that "many great and precious truths" have been omitted from the Bible as we know it today.

Doctrine and Covenants

Doctrine and Covenants is a collection of writings purported to be a revelation given by God to Joseph Smith (although the last revelation was given to Brigham

Young). It contains 136 chapters, and each chapter is divided into verses. The language appears to someone familiar with literature and literary style to be a strange hodgepodge of King James language, Elizabethan poetical vocabulary, and nineteenth-century romanticism.

These revelations supposedly deal with doctrines of the true church. Within its covers are found the doctrines of celestial marriage, baptism for the dead, and polygamy, none of which are taught in either the Bible or *The Book of Mormon*. In fact, *The Book of Mormon* denounces polygamy with labels such as "grosser crime," "abominable," "wickedness," and "whoredom."

Although many of the revelations in *Doctrine and Covenants* are of a general nature and are applicable to the entire body of believers, some were specifically addressed to individuals and dealt with specific problems. One revelation (Section 19) was given in the spring of 1830 and commanded the printer to be paid for printing *The Book of Mormon's* first edition. Sections 20-23 deal with the establishment of the Church of Jesus Christ of Latter Day Saints in April of 1830, and Section 3 describes the calamity which occurred when 116 pages of the transcribed manuscript of *The Book of Mormon* were lost. Later in this book we will return to these sections in a historical reconstruction of the events of that fateful period and what we believe really happened.

Perhaps the best-known section of *Doctrine and Covenants* is Section 132, which also concerns an individual in the church. This is the famous section on plural marriage and includes God's command to Emma, Smith's first wife, to welcome her husband's new wives or face eternal destruction. Others who have studied the early activities of the Mormon Church have produced convincing testimony to the effect that Joseph had already married at least twelve other wives *before* the date of the revelation contained in *Doctrine and Covenants.*[1]

In 1890, President Woodruff of the Mormon Church issued a Manifesto (referred to previously) denouncing the practice of plural marriage. Strangely, this Manifesto was incorporated into *Doctrine and Covenants,* and, without any attempt within the volume to reconcile its pronouncement with the opposite pronouncement to Smith, it stands at the end of the volume as a silent testimony to the persuasive ability of pragmatism on the "everlasting" revelations. (The United States government gave the Mormons an ultimatum—either stop practicing polygamy or leave the country—and Woodruff's "revelation" appeared soon afterward.)

The Pearl of Great Price

The Pearl of Great Price is a bridge between *The Book of Mormon* and *Doctrine and Covenants.* While not entirely a sacred history (as is the former) and not entirely a compilation of latter-day commands (as is the latter), *The Pearl of Great Price* is a combination of the two. It consists of "The Articles of Faith" by Smith, portions of "The History of Joseph Smith the Prophet," "The Book of Abraham," and two portions of Joseph's "translation" (enlargement and modification) of the Bible: Matthew 24 and Genesis 1 - 6.

"The Articles of Faith," unlike some portions of inspired Mormon literature, are still held as authoritative today, and contain (among other things) comments on the canon of Mormon revelation and the importance (or lack of it) of the Bible in Mormon theology. Concerning the Bible, Article 8 states: "We believe the Bible to be the word of God as far as it is translated correctly; we also believe the Book of Mormon to be the word of God." Note that, while the authority of the Bible is qualified, no such restriction applies to *The Book of Mormon*. It is also important to note that what Smith considered to be "translated correctly" is vastly different from the considerations taken into account by eminent Greek and Hebrew scholars. For example, Joseph "translated" the Book of Genesis and added a prophecy of his own coming! He said that Genesis 50 should contain the words, "And that seer will I bless. . .and his name shall be called Joseph, and it shall be after the name of his father. . .for the thing which the Lord shall bring forth by his hand shall bring my people unto salvation" (v. 33).

The portion of *The Pearl of Great Price* called "The History of Joseph Smith the Prophet" is just that: the history of his "calling" by God to restore the true church to the earth. It includes, among other things, an account of Smith's first vision (quoted in our Chapter 1), subsequent visions, and revelations from the heavens (through God and angels). It forms what might be considered Joseph's credentials, establishing his supposed authority as God's spokesman.

"The Book of Moses" is that portion of *The Pearl of Great Price* which copies Smith's "Revised Version" of the King James Bible from Genesis. In contrast to the Bible (the product of careful scholarship), "The Book of Moses" introduces various novel teachings. Included among these are such concepts as: 1) Adam's sin was beneficial in that without it there would have been no human procreation; 2) humans' souls existed before birth; 3) Adam was baptized by immersion; and 4) Satan offered to die to redeem mankind.

The final section of *The Pearl of Great Price* that will be discussed here is known as "The Book of Abraham,"

which purports to be a translation of Egyptian papyri—
said by Joseph to be "reformed Egyptian hieroglyphics."
(Unlike *The Book of Mormon*, "The Book of Abraham"
teaches polytheism very clearly, even stating that in the
beginning "they [the gods] said. . . .")

Modern research has done much to uncover the true
source of "The Book of Abraham." It had been the contention of the Mormon Church until 1967 that the
papyrus materials which Joseph Smith had translated
had been destroyed in the Chicago fire of 1871. With the
originals safely out of reach of reputable scholars' ex-
aminations, the Mormon hierarchy could remain
unruffled by critics' contentions that the book was not
what Joseph Smith had claimed.

However, in 1967 it became known that some of the
papyri that Joseph had "translated" were lying in a room
at the Metropolitan Museum—available for the scrutiny
of Egyptologists who could verify once and for all its
relationship to "The Book of Abraham." The papyri
were given to the LDS Church in Salt Lake City, and the
task of translating them was begun after some delay. Dr.
Hugh Nibley of Brigham Young University was
somewhat acquainted with Egyptian hieroglyphics, but
according to a letter said, "I don't consider myself an
Egyptologist at all, and don't intend to get involved. . . ."[2] Instead, he was instrumental in providing
copies of the papyri for Dee Jay Nelson, a Mormon who
did have the qualifications for making the translation
and who made his translation public in 1968.

Dr. Nibley stated concerning Nelson's translation,
". . . a conscientious piece of work for which the Latter-
day Saints owe a debt of gratitude to Mr. Dee Jay
Nelson. . . . This is a conscientious and courageous piece
of work. . . supplying students with a usable and reliable
translation of the available papyri that once belonged to

Joseph Smith."[3] Nelson's conclusion, based on his translation and corroborated by Prof. Richard A. Parker of Brown University and Klaus Baer of the University of Chicago, is that the papyri contain instructions for wrapping the Egyptian sacred book of "breathings" with the mummy it was found with, and has nothing at all to do with Abraham, the Bible, Mormonism, or the God of the Jews.[4]

The conclusion of objective study can only be that *The Pearl of Great Price* is not even remotely related to the God of the Bible and historic Christianity. (See Appendix 1 for Professor Nelson's authoritative conclusions.)

The Book of Mormon

The Book of Mormon, the last of the three Mormon sacred books, is the topic of the remaining chapters of this book. Briefly, *The Book of Mormon* is an account of two great migrations to North and South America by Semites—the "Jaredites" and the followers of "Lehi," a Jew. The Jaredites were supposed to have lived near the Tower of Babel and to have crossed the ocean to Central America in 2250 B.C. aboard eight barges.

After settling in Central America (with animals never known to have been on this continent), the Jaredites began to fight among themselves, and in one battle two million men, plus their wives and children, were slain. Finally, only Coriantumr, Shiz, and Ether were left of the whole race. Ether, a prophet, wrote the history of the Jaredites and witnessed the final battle between Coriantumr and Shiz, in which Shiz was decapitated and then "after that he [headless] had struggled for breath, he died" (Ether 15:31). Coriantumr survived despite wounds and lived for "nine moons." Ether inscribed the history of the Jaredites on 24 plates, and thus ended the Jaredites' existence.

The second, and far more important, group of Semites to travel from the Old World to the New consisted of Lehi and his descendants. Lehi was descended from the Israelite tribe of Manasseh, having left Jerusalem in 600 B.C. because of his prophecies of doom and the persecution he suffered. He, his wife, and their four sons moved to the region of the Red Sea, and, once they had traveled to the ocean, sailed to the west coast of South America. Lehi had in his possession a set of brass plates containing the Pentateuch (the five books of Moses), prophecies, and Lehi's genealogy. The trip was aided by a mariner's compass which Lehi had found (but which, unfortunately for the credibility of the story, was not invented until the 1100's A.D.!). Two of Lehi's sons were continually disobedient (Laman and Lemuel) and were subsequently cursed by God and thus received black skins. The dark or red-skinned American Indians are said to be descendants of Lamanites, as the descendants of Laman are called. Lehi's two other sons' descendants, led by Nephi, remained faithful to God. They called themselves Nephites and moved into Central and North America. In fulfillment of a prophecy made by Nephi, Jesus Christ supposedly came down from heaven in 34 A.D. and taught the faithful Nephites baptism, communion, and the greater part of the Sermon on the Mount.

In 385 A.D. the Nephites and Lamanites battled for a final time near the hill Cumorah (near Joseph Smith's hometown of Palmyra, New York) and all the Nephites except for Mormon's son, Moroni, were killed.

Mormon had been recording the history of his people on golden plates in the tradition of other scribes who had kept records on plates, starting with Nephi himself. After revising the larger plates and then annexing this revision to the smaller plates, Mormon hid them in the ground near the hill. After the battle, Moroni added the books of Ether and Moroni. In 421 A.D. Moroni buried these in the hill too. Moroni returned to the hill as an angel from 1823-27 and gave these plates to Joseph Smith.

According to Joseph Smith, Jr., "I told the brethren that *The Book of Mormon* was the most correct of any book on earth, and the keystone of our religion, and a man would get nearer to God by abiding its precepts than by any other book."[5]

Mormon apostle Orson Pratt has said of this work:

This book must be either true or false. If true, it is one of the most important messages ever sent from God. . . . If false, it is one of the most cunning, wicked, bold, deep-laid impositions ever palmed upon the world, calculated to deceive and ruin millions. . . . The nature of the message in the Book of Mormon is such that, if true, no one can possibly be saved and reject it; if false, no one can possibly be saved and receive it. . . . If, after a rigid examination, it be found an imposition, it should be extensively published to the world as such; the evidences and arguments on which the imposture was detected, should be clearly and logically stated, that those who have been sincerely yet unfortunately deceived, may perceive the nature of the deception, and be reclaimed, and that those who continue to publish the delusion, may be exposed and silenced, not by physical force, neither by persecutions, bare assertions, nor ridicule, but by strong and powerful arguments—by evidences adduced from scripture and reason. . . . But on the other hand, if investigations should prove the Book of Mormon true . . . the American and English nations should utterly reject both the Popish and Protestant ministry, together with all the churches which have been built up by them or that have sprung from them, as being entirely destitute of authority. . . .[6]

We accept the challenge of Orson Pratt, and we believe that there is more than sufficient evidence for showing that *The Book of Mormon* is not God's revelation to man and that Joseph Smith is not the founder of the restored church. We believe that the evidence for these assertions is overwhelming and can convince a sincere reader that Solomon Spalding's novel was pirated and revised and is known today as *The Book of Mormon*. Much of the information in these pages has been mentioned from time to time ever since Spalding's death and the emergence of the Mormon Church. However, to our knowledge no one has previously compiled the volume or weight of evidence that we have, and no one has previously produced this added proof: *The Book of Mormon* (or *Manuscript Found*) in Solomon Spalding's own handwriting.

NOTES

1. Jerald and Sandra Tanner, *Mormonism: Shadow or Reality* (Modern Microfilm Co., Salt Lake City, 1972), pp. 202ff.
2. Ibid., p. 308.
3. Ibid., p. 310.
4. Ibid., p. 317.
5. Joseph Fielding Smith, *Teachings of the Prophet Joseph Smith* (Deseret Books, Salt Lake City, 1958), p. 194.
6. Tanner, p. 50.

The
Spalding
Saga

Solomon Spalding was born in Ashford, Connecticut, on February 20, 1761, the third of ten children. After he completed his early schooling he attended the Plainfield Academy. There, according to his brother John, he was near the top of his class. His father, Josiah, joined the rebel forces during the Revolutionary War, and Solomon followed him on January 8, 1778, by joining Col. Obadiah Johnson's regiment as a private under Captain John Williams. He also worked on his parents' farm intermittently.

After the war, Spalding studied law with Judge Zephaniah Swift in Windham, Connecticut. Later he entered prestigious Dartmouth College in preparation for the ministry and graduated in 1785 (after entering as a sophomore) with a master's degree.

Spalding became associated with the Windham Congregational Association on October 9, 1787 (at that time the Congregational denomination was one of the most widespread of all denominations in the eastern United States). He was ordained in that denomination and ministered as an evangelist for about a decade. Because of ill health, he turned down numerous offers to become a regular pastor of a congregation. In 1795 he married Matilda Sabine.

Spalding's Reverses

Soon after this, Spalding and his wife moved to Cherry Valley, New York, and joined another brother, Josiah, in his mercantile business. Solomon Spalding also ran the Cherry Valley Academy and was its first principal. He preached less and less frequently until finally, as a result of marital problems and poor health, and assailed by theological doubts, he terminated his public ministry.

In 1799, the store was moved sixteen miles to Richfield (now known as Richfield Springs). Almost immediately the Spalding brothers Josiah and Solomon bought large tracts of land in Ohio and Pennsylvania with the intention of selling them in smaller portions and realizing a profit. In about 1809 Solomon and Matilda Spalding moved to Salem (now known as Conneaut), a small village in northeastern Ohio, in order to superintend the land. In addition to his supervisorial responsibilities, Solomon worked with a Henry Lake in maintaining an iron forge for General Keyes.

Spalding's health deteriorated further, and to occupy his leisure time he began writing novels. When the War of 1812 began, the Spaldings' business failed.

In 1812 Solomon and Matilda moved to Pittsburgh in

hopes of printing and selling his *second* novel (*Manuscript Found*) in order to pay off their debts. (In Pittsburgh they also ran a small store.) Very short of funds and with rapidly deteriorating health, Spalding and his wife moved to Amity (not far from Pittsburgh), a less expensive community with a climate more conducive to promoting his return to health. The couple operated a nonalcoholic "temperance tavern" there.

The climate did not restore Spalding's health, and his final illness, lasting five or six weeks, culminated in his death on October 20, 1816.

Spalding the Novelist

According to his contemporaries, Solomon Spalding was a romantic. He loved stories of adventure and romantic history and had an almost-insatiable desire to know the history of the American continents—a history which at that time was almost unknown. He seemed to consider himself a fair novelist and dedicated many hours to writing his own "history" of the Americas. He spent many additional hours sharing his literary products with his friends, neighbors, and almost anyone who would listen.

Unfortunately, others did not share his conviction that he was a great novelist. Contemporaries tolerated his "readings" and tried to give him constructive criticism. However, instead of being known as "Solomon the novelist," he became known by some as "Old Came-to-Pass"—after one of his favorite literary phrases ("and it came to pass").

Spalding devoted himself primarily to two separate but similar novels. The first novel, and his first attempt at writing, was called *Manuscript Story* and was experimental. Through the criticisms of his acquaintances and his experiments in *Manuscript Story*, Spalding was able to abandon his first attempt before it was completed and to use what he had learned to prepare a new novel, *Manuscript Found*.

Spalding's acquaintances and family later stated that this second novel had been stolen from the printshop to which it had been taken in Pittsburgh and that it resurfaced in 1830 as *The Book of Mormon* (with some modifications and revisions). We hope to show through a careful examination of the lives of Solomon Spalding, Joseph Smith, Jr., and Sidney Rigdon that this is indeed what happened. Let us now look at contemporary testimony concerning Solomon Spalding and his *Manuscript Found*.

Statements of the Eight Witnesses

John Spalding, one of Solomon Spalding's brothers, has left us with two of his own statements and one from his wife, Martha. His first statement concerns the period during Solomon's life at Conneaut, Ohio (1809-12). John Spalding said:

Solomon Spalding was born in Ashford, Conn., in 1761, and in early life contracted a taste for literary pursuits. After he left school, he entered Plainfield Academy, where he made great proficiency in study, and excelled most of his classmates. He next commenced the study of law, in Windham county, in which he made little progress, having in the meantime turned his attention to religious subjects. He soon after entered Dartmouth College, with the intention of qualifying himself for the ministry, where he obtained the degree of A.M., and was afterwards regularly ordained. After preaching three or four years, he gave it up, removed to Cherry Valley, N.Y., and commenced the mercantile business, in company with his brother

Josiah. In a few years he failed in business, and in the year 1809 removed to Conneaut, in Ohio. The year following, I removed to Ohio, and found him engaged in building a forge. I made him a visit in about three years after, and found that he had failed, and was considerably involved in debt. He then told me he had been writing a book, which he intended to have printed, the avails of which he thought would enable him to pay all his debts. The book was entitled the "Manuscript Found", of which he read to me many passages. It was an historical romance of the first settlers of America, endeavoring to show that the American Indians are the descendants of the Jews, or the lost tribes. It gave a detailed account of their journey from Jerusalem, by land and sea, till they arrived in America, under the command of Nephi[a] and Lehi.[b] They afterwards had quarrels and contentions, and seperated[c] into two distinct nations, one of which he denominated Nephites, and the other Lamanites. Cruel and bloody wars ensued, in which great multitudes were slain. They buried their dead in large heaps, which caused the mounds so common in this country. Their arts, sciences and civilization were brought into view in order to account for all the curious antiquities found in various parts of North and South America. I have recently read the Book of Mormon and to my great surprise I find it nearly the same historical matter, names, & c., as they were in my brother's writings. I well remember that he wrote in the old style, and commenced about every sentence with "And it came to pass," or "Now it came to pass," the same as in the Book of Mormon, and according to the best of my recollection and belief, it is the same as my brother Solomon wrote, with the exception of the

---

[a]Nephi is a name Spalding obtained from Second Maccabbees 1:36 (A book of the Apocrypha).

[b]Lehi in Hebrew means "jawbone of an ass."

[c]All quotations in this book are reproduced exactly, including spelling and punctuation as shown in the original documents.

religious matter. By what means it has fallen into the
hands of Joseph Smith, Jr., I am unable to determine.
      (Signed)
      John Spalding[1]

John Spalding made a similar statement in *The
Yankee Mahomet* (quoted in *American Review*, June
1851, p. 554), which was corroborated by his son Daniel
and many other acquaintances:

Solomon Spalding was born in Ashford, Conn., A.D.
1761. He graduated at Dartmouth College, and was
afterwards regularly ordained a minister. After
preaching three or four years, he gave up his
profession, and commenced mercantile business, in
partnership with his brother Josiah, in Cherry Valley,
N.Y., where he soon failed. In 1809 he removed to
Conneaut, Ohio, where he engaged himself in
building an iron forge; but in this business also he soon
failed. Casting about him for some method of retriev-
ing his losses, he conceived the design of writing a
historical romance upon a subject then much mooted
in the scientific world, the origin of the Indian tribes.
This design he carried into execution between 1809
and 1812, and the produce of his labors was a novel
entitled the 'Manuscript Found'. In this work he
mentioned that the American continent was colonized
by Lehi, the son of Japheth, who sailed from Chaldea
soon after the great dispersion, and landed near the
isthmus of Darien. Lehi's descendants, who were
styled Jaredites, spread gradually to the north, bearing
with them the remains of antediluvian science, and
building those cities the ruins of which we see in
Central America, and the fortifications which are
scattered along the Cordilleras. Long after this, Nephi,
of the tribe of Joseph, emigrated to America with a
large portion of the ten tribes whom Shalmanezer led
away from Palestine, and scattered among the Midian
cities. This remnant of Joseph was soon after its arrival
divided into two nations, the Nephites and the

Lamanites. These nations made war constantly against each other, and in the year A.D. 420, a great battle was fought in western New York, which terminated in the destruction of the armies of both the belligerent parties, and the annihilation of their power. One man only was left; Moroni, the son of Mormon, who had the records of the Nephites near Conneaut, Ohio, previously at his death.

Concerning this same period in Spalding's life (1809-12), when he lived in Conneaut, Ohio, John's wife (Solomon's sister-in-law), Martha, affirmed:

I was personally acquainted with Solomon Spalding, about twenty years ago. I was at his house a short time before he left Conneaut; he was then writing an historical novel founded upon the first settlers of America. He represented them as an enlightened and warlike people. He had for many years contended that the aborigines of America were the descendants of some of the lost tribes of Israel, and this idea he carried out in the book in question. The lapse of time which has intervened, prevents my recollecting but few of the leading incidents of his writings; but the names of Nephi and Lehi are yet fresh in my memory, as being the principal heroes of his tale. They were officers of the company which first came off from Jerusalem. He gave a particular account of their journey by land and sea, till they arrived in America, after which disputes arose between the chiefs, which caused them to separate into different bands, one of which was called Lamanites, and the other Nephites. Between these were recounted tremendous battles, which frequently covered the ground with the slain; and their being buried in large heaps was the cause of the numerous mounds in the country. Some of these people he represented as being very large. I have read the Book of Mormon[d] which has brought fresh to my

---

[d] "Mormon" is a classical Greek word of which one meaning is "monster."

recollection the writings of Solomon Spalding; and I have no manner of doubt that the historical part of it is the same that I read and heard read more than twenty years ago. The old, obsolete style, and the phrases of "and it came to pass," & c., are the same.

(Signed)
Martha Spalding[2]

Josiah Spalding, the brother with whom Solomon worked at the mercantile business, recalled in later years that Solomon's widow had told him "that my brother continued his history of the civilized nation and the progress of the war until the triumph of the savages to the destruction of the civilized government."[3] Interestingly, this is precisely the ending found in *The Book of Mormon*!

During this same period in Solomon's life (1809-12), he tried to make a financially successful enterprise of a forge in Conneaut. His partner was Henry Lake, and during 1811 one of his employees was John N. Miller. Miller stated that he was very familiar with Spalding's second novel, *Manuscript Found,* and that his later acquaintance with *The Book of Mormon* confirmed his belief that the two books were essentially one and the same. He said:

In the year 1811, I was in the employ of Henry Lake and Solomon Spaulding, at Conneaut, engaged in rebuilding a forge. While there, I boarded and lodged in the family of said Spaulding for several months. I was soon introduced to the manuscripts of Spaulding, and persued them as often as I had leisure. He had written two or three books or pamphlets on different subjects; but that which more particularly drew my attention was one which he called the "Manuscript Found." From this he would frequently read some humorous passages to the company present. It purported to be the history of the first settlement of America, before discovered by Columbus. He brought them off from Jerusalem, under their leaders; detailing their travels by land and water, their manners, customs, laws, wars, & c. He said that he designed it as an historical novel, and that in after years it would be believed by many people as much as the history of England. He soon after failed in business, and told me he would retire from the din of his creditors, finish his book and have it published, which would enable him to pay his debts and support his family. He soon after removed to Pittsburgh, as I understood.

I have recently examined the Book of Mormon, and find in it the writings of Solomon Spaulding, from beginning to end, but mixed up with Scripture and other religious matter, which I did not meet with in the "Manuscript Found." Many of the passages in the Mormon book are verbatim from Spaulding, and others in part. The names of Nephi, Lehi, Moroni,[e] and in fact all the principal names, are brought fresh to my recollection by the Golden Bible. When Spaulding divested his history of its fabulous names, by a verbal explanation, he landed his people near the Straits of Darien, which I am very confident he called Zarahemla; they were marched about that country for a length of time, in which wars and great bloodshed ensued; he brought them across North America in a northeast direction.

(Signed)
John N. Miller[4]

Mr. Miller, interestingly , expressed the opinion that many of the passages of *Manuscript Found* were humorous, even after he later read the Golden Bible. Considering Spaulding's addiction to the phrase "and it came to pass" and his stilted, though romantic, writing style, the adjective "humorous" seems a natural appellation for

---

[e]"Moroni" was the name of a famous Italian painter in the 1500's.

a story that at the time of Miller's familiarity with it, was never claimed to be anything more than a historical novel. All the many people who knew of Spalding's literary efforts recognized that even the most serious scenes in his book were, after all, nothing but fiction which Solomon Spalding hoped would sound plausible.

The statement of Artemas Cunningham was published in 1834 and distributed publicly in an attempt to assert the true authorship of *The Book of Mormon*. Cunningham traveled to the Spalding residence in October of 1811 to try to obtain money owed him by Spalding. He declared:

> In the month of October, 1811, I went from the township of Madison to Conneaut, for the purpose of securing a debt due me from Solomon Spalding. I tarried with him nearly two days, for the purpose of accomplishing my object, which I was finally unable to do. I found him destitute of the means of paying his debts. His only hope of ever paying his debts appeared to be upon the sale of a book which he had been writing. He endeavored to convince me from the nature and character of the work, that it would meet with a ready sale. Before showing me his manuscripts, he went into a verbal relation of its outlines, saying that it was a fabulous or romantic history of the first settlement of this country, and as it purported to have been a record found buried in the earth, or in a cave, he had adopted the ancient or Scripture style of writing. He then presented his manuscripts, when we sat down, and spent a good share of the night in reading them, and conversing upon them. I well remember the name of Nephi, which appeared to be the principal hero of the story. The frequent repetition of the phrase, "I Neph," I recollect as distinctly as though it was but yesterday, although the general features of the story have passed from my memory, through the lapse of twenty-two years. He attempted to

account for the numerous antiquities which are found upon this continent, and remarked that, after this generation had passed away, his account of the first inhabitants of America would be considered as authentic as any other history. The Mormon Bible I have partially examined, and am fully of the opinion that Solomon Spaulding had written its outlines before he left Conneaut.[5]

Of the eight witnesses whose testimony confirms the existence of *Manuscript Found* in Conneaut, Ohio, during the period of 1809-12, perhaps one of the most important is Henry Lake, Solomon's business partner at the iron forge. He borrowed a copy of Smith's "Golden Bible" some twenty years after his partnership with Solomon, and thereby chanced on the same manuscript he had known so well in Conneaut.

According to Henry Lake:

I left the State of New York, late in the year 1810, and arrived at this place [Conneaut], about the first of January following. Soon after my arrival, I formed a copartnership with Solomon Spaulding, for the purpose of rebuilding a forge which he had commenced a year or two before. He very frequently read to me from a manuscript which he was writing which he entitled the "Manuscript Found," and which he represented as being found in this town. I spent many hours in hearing him read said writings, and became well acquainted with its contents. He wished me to assist him in getting his production printed, alleging that a book of that kind would meet with a rapid sale. I designed doing so, but the forge not meeting our anticipations, we failed in business, when I declined having anything to do with the publication of the book. This book represented the American Indians as the descendants of the lost tribes, gave account of their leaving Jerusalem, their contentions and wars, which were many and great. One time, when he was reading to me the tragic account of Laban, I pointed out to him what I considered an inconsistency, which he promised to correct: but by referring to the Book of Mormon, I find, to my surprise, that it stands there just as he read it to me then.[f] Some months ago, I borrowed the Golden Bible, put it into my pocket, carried it home, and thought no more of it. About a week after, my wife found the book in my coat pocket, as it hung up, and commenced reading it aloud as I lay upon the bed. She had not read twenty minutes, till I was astonished to find the same passages in it that Spaulding had read to me more than twenty years before, from his "Manuscript Found." Since that, I have more fully examined the said Golden Bible, and have no hesitation in saying that the historical part of it is principally, if not wholly, taken from the "Manuscript Found." I well recollect telling Mr. Spaulding that the so frequent use of the words "And it came to pass," "Now it came to pass," rendered it ridiculous. Spaulding left here in 1812, and I furnished him the means to carry him to Pittsburgh, where he said he would get the book printed and pay me. But I never heard any more from him or his writings, till I saw them in the Book of Mormon.

(Signed)
Henry Lake[6]

The seventh of the eight witnesses to this period of the manuscript's history is Aaron Wright. Wright was one of the earliest settlers in Conneaut and was the Justice of the Peace there for many years. The Public Library at Conneaut still has his Docket Book on file as a

---

[f]In First Nephi 3:28, 29 (*Book of Mormon*), Nephi says, ". . . Laman and Lemuel did speak many hard words unto us, their younger brothers, and they did smite us even with a rod. And it came to pass as they smote us with a rod. . . ." Then an angel immediately says, "Why do ye smite your younger brother with a rod?" The inconsistency Mr. Lake remembered all those years was that Nephi spoke of *brothers* (plural) while the angel spoke of only one brother.

historical artifact. When *The Book of Mormon* was read during a public meeting in Conneaut in 1832, it was Justice Wright who exclaimed, "Old Come-to-Pass has come to life again!" A very droll man, Wright always said what was on his mind and usually could be counted on to get to the heart of matters. He stated:

> I first became acquainted with Solomon Spaulding in 1808 or '9, when he commenced building a forge on Conneaut Creek. When at his house, one day, he showed and read to me a history he was writing, of the lost tribes of Israel, purporting that they were the first settlers of America, and that the Indians were their descendants. He traced their journey from Jerusalem to America, as it is given in the Book of Mormon, excepting the religious matter. The historical part of the Book of Mormon I know to be the same as I read and heard read from the writings of Spaulding, more than twenty years ago; the names, more especially, are the same without any alteration. He told me his object was to account for all the fortifications, &c., to be found in this county, and said that in time it would be fully believed by all, except learned men and historians. I, once anticipated reading his writings in print, but little expected to see them in a new Bible. Spaulding had many other manuscripts, which I expect to see when Smith translates his other plate. In conclusion, I will observe that the names of, and most of the historical part of the Book of Mormon, were as familiar to me before I read it, as most modern history. If it is not Spaulding's writing, it is the same as he wrote; and if Smith was inspired, I think it was by the same spirit that Spaulding was, which confessed to be the love of money.
>
> (Signed)
> Aaron Wright[7]

Dr. Nahum Howard was the town doctor at Conneaut during the period Solomon lived there, and quite likely tended the man when he was ill, which was frequently. Dr. Howard's comments, though short, corroborate those of the first seven witnesses. He said:

> I first became acquainted with Solomon Spaulding, in December, 1810. After that time, I frequently saw him at his house, and also at my house. I once, in conversation with him, expressed a surprise at not having any account of the inhabitants once in this country, who erected the old forts, mounds, &c. He then told me that he was writing a history of that race of people; and afterwards frequently showed me his writings, which I read. I have lately read the Book of Mormon, and believe it to be the same as Spaulding wrote, except the religious part. He told me that he intended to get his writings published in Pittsburgh, and he thought that in one century from that time, it would be believed as much as any other history.
>   (Signed)
>   Nahum Howard
>   August 1833, Conneaut[8]

The above testimonies should certainly constitute sufficient evidence to cause any honest reader to question the divine origins of *The Book of Mormon*. The voices of Spalding's friends and relatives who saw the novel in its infancy are united. All agree that *Manuscript Found*, Spalding's second novel, is *The Book of Mormon*. There is further testimony to this effect from those who considered themselves responsible spokesmen on the subject (see Appendix 4 for additional testimony). Yet there were still others who swore so adamantly that Spalding was the source of *The Book of Mormon* that Sidney Rigdon, evidently the mastermind behind the plagiaristic plot, felt that he had to respond to the charges. Let us look at those charges and Sidney's response.

Matilda, Solomon Spalding's wife, has provided a lengthy testimony to the facts as she saw them in the case between her late husband's novel and the fledgling Church of Jesus Christ of Latter Day Saints. The following was her published statement in *The Boston Recorder* of 1839:

ORIGIN OF THE "BOOK OF MORMON," OR "GOLDEN BIBLE."

As this book has excited much attention, and has been put by a certain new sect in place of the sacred Scriptures, I deem it a duty which I owe to the public to state what I know touching its origin.

That its claims to a divine origin are wholly unfounded, needs no proof to a mind unperverted by the grossest delusions. That any sane person should rank it any higher than any other merely human composition is a matter of the greatest astonishment; yet it is received as divine by some who dwell in enlightened New England, and even by those who have sustained the character of devoted Christians. Learning recently that Mormonism has found its way into a church in Massachusetts, and has impregnated some of its members with some of its gross delusions, so that excommunication has become necessary, I am determined to delay no longer doing what I can to strip the mask from this monster of sin, and to lay open this pit of abomination. Rev. Solomon Spalding, to whom I was united in marriage in early life, was a graduate of Dartmouth college, and was distinguised for a lively imagination and a great fondness for history. At the time of our marriage he resided in Cherry Valley, New York. From this place we removed to New Salem, Ashtabula county, Ohio, sometimes called Conneaut, as it is situated upon Conneaut creek. Shortly after our removal to this place, his health sunk, and he was laid aside from active labors. In the town of New Salem there are numerous mounds and forts, supposed by many to be the dilapidated dwellings and fortifications of a race now extinct. These ancient relics arrest the attention of the new settlers, and become objects of research for the curious. Numerous implements were found, and other articles, evincing great skill in the arts. Mr. Spalding being an educated man and passionately fond of history, took a lively interest in these developments of antiquity, and in order to beguile the hours of retirement and furnish employment for his lively imagination, he conceived the idea of giving an historical sketch of this long lost race. Their extreme antiquity of course would let him to write in the most ancient style;[g] and as the Old Testament is the most ancient book in the world, he imitated its style[g] as nearly as possible. His sole object in writing this historical romance was to amuse himself and his neighbors. This was about the year 1812. Hull's surrender at Detroit occurred near the same time, and I recollect the date well from that circumstance. As he progressed in his narrative, the neighbors would come in from time to time to hear portions of it read, and a great interest in the work was excited among them.

It is claimed to have been written by one of the lost nation, and to have been recovered from the earth, and assumed the title of "Manuscript Found". The neighbors would often inquire how Mr. Spalding progressed in "Deciphering" the "Manuscript", and when he had a sufficient portion prepared, he would inform them and they would assemble to hear it read. He was enabled from his acquaintance with the classics and ancient history to introduce many singular names, which were particularly noticed by the people, and could be easily recognized by them. Mr. Solomon Spalding had a brother, Mr. John Spalding, residing in the place at the time, who was perfectly familiar with this work, and repeatedly heard the whole of it read.

From New Salem we removed to Pittsburgh, Pa. Here we found a friend in the person of Mr. Patterson, an editor of a newspaper. He exhibited his manuscript to Mr. P., who was very much pleased with it, and

---

[g] Elizabethan English was also the style of *The Book of Mormon*.

borrowed it for perusal. He retained it for a long time and informed Mr. S. that if he would make out a title page and preface, he would publish it, and it would be a source of profit.[h]

This Mr. S. refused to do, for reasons which I cannot now state. Sidney Rigdon, one of the leaders and founders of the sect, who had figured so largely in the history of the Mormons, was at this time connected[i] with the printing office of Mr. Patterson, as he is well known in that region, and as Rigdon himself has frequently stated. Here he had ample opportunity to become acquainted with Mr. Spalding's manuscript, and to copy it if he chose. It was a matter of notoriety and interest to all who were connected with the printing establishment. At length the manuscript was returned to its author,[j] and soon after we removed to Amity, Washington County, Pa., where Mr. S. deceased in 1816. The manuscript then fell into my hands, and was carefully preserved. It has frequently been examined by my daughter, Mrs. McKinstry, of Monson, Mass., with whom I now reside, and by other friends. After the "Book of Mormon" came out, a copy of it was taken to New Salem, the place of Mr. Spalding's former residence, and the very place where the "Manuscript Found" was written. A Mormon preacher appointed a meeting there, and in the meeting read and repeated copious extracts from the "Book of Mormon". The historical part was immediately recognized by the older inhabitants before. Mr. John Spalding was present, who is an eminently pious man, and recognized perfectly the work of his brother. He was amazed and afflicted that it should have perverted to so wicked a purpose. His grief found vent in a flood of tears, and he arose on the spot and expressed in the meeting his deep sorrow and regret

---

[h]As other testimonies recorded, this money would have been welcomed, enabling Spalding to pay his debts.

[i]Perhaps as a part-time tanner.

[j]This was a guess on her part.

that the writings of his sainted brother should be used for a purpose so vile and shocking. The excitement in New Salem became so great that the inhabitants had a meeting and deputed Dr. Philaster Hurlbut, one of their number, to repair to this place and to obtain from me the original manuscript of Mr. Spalding, for the purpose of comparing it with the Mormon Bible to satisfy their own minds and to prevent their friends from embracing an error so delusive.

This was in the year 1834. Dr. Hurlbut brought with him an introduction and request for the manuscript, signed by Messrs. Henry Lake, Aaron Wright and others, with all of whom I was acquainted, as they were my neighbors when I resided in New Salem.

I am sure that nothing could grieve my husband more, were he living, than the use which has been made of his work. The air of antiquity which has been thrown about the composition, doubtless suggested the idea of converting it to purpose of delusion. Thus an historical romance, with the addition of a few pious expressions and extracts from the sacred Scriptures, has been constructed into a new Bible, and palmed off upon a company of poor deluded fanatics as divine.

I have given the previous narration, that this work of deep deception and wickedness may be searched to the foundation and its author exposed to the contempt and execration he so justly deserves.

(Signed)
Matilda Davison

Rev. Solomon Spalding was the first husband of the narrator of the above history. Since his decease she has been married to a second husband, by the name of Davidson. She is now residing in this place, is a woman of irreproachable character, and a humble Christian, and her testimony is worthy of implicit confidence.

A. Ely, D.D.
Pastor of the Congregational Church, Monson.
D.R. Austin, principal of Monson Academy.[9]
Monson, March 1, 1839.

Mrs. Davison's statement was published in *The Boston Recorder* in 1839. The testimony has been disputed by Mormons and its reliability has been carefully examined and weighed. We have carefully investigated the matter and have come to the conclusion that, although some of Mrs. Davison's details are faulty (probably because of poor memory or lack of communication from her husband), her testimony is nevertheless essentially in harmony with the bulk of the testimony we have already examined (see Appendix 3).

Rigdon's Denial

Sidney Rigdon was at this time a Mormon of nine years and one of its most vocal spokesmen. He quickly jumped not only to a defense of Mormonism, but to his own defense as well. His reply to Mrs. Davison's statement was written on May 27, 1839, and read as follows:

> Messrs. Bartlett & Sullivan:—In your paper of the 18th inst., I see a letter signed by somebody calling herself Matilda Davison. It is only necessary to say, in relation to the whole story about Spaulding's writings being in the hands of Mr. Patterson, who was in Pittsburgh, and who is said to have kept a printing office, and my saying that I was connected in the said office, &c., &c., is the most base of lies, without even the shadow of truth. There was no man by the name of Patterson, during my residence at Pittsburgh, who had a printing office; what might have been before I lived there I know not. Mr. Robert Patterson, I was told, had owned a printing office before I lived in that city, but had been unfortunate in business, and failed before my residence there. This Mr. Patterson, who was a Presbyterian preacher, I had a very slight acquaintance with during my residence in Pittsburgh. He was then acting under an agency, in the book and station-

ary business, and was the owner of no property of any kind, printing office or anything else, during the time I resided in the city.[k]

If I were to say that I ever heard of the Rev. Solomon Spaulding and his wife, until Dr. P. Hulbert wrote his lie about me, I should be a liar like unto themselves. Why was not the testimony of Mr. Patterson obtained to give force to this shameful tale of lies?[l] The only reason is, that he was not a fit tool for them to work with; he would not lie for them; for, if he were called on, he would testify to what I have here said.

Let me here, gentlemen, give a history of this Dr. P. Hulbert and his associates who aided in getting up and propagating this batch of lies.

I have seen and heard, at one time and another, by the persecutors and haters of the truth, a great deal about the eminent physician, Dr. Hulbert. I never thought the matter worthy of notice, nor probably ever should, had it not made its appearance in your paper, or some one of equal respectability. And I believe, gentlemen, had you have known the whole history of this budget of lies, it would never have found a place in your paper. But to my history.

This said Doctor was never a physician at any time, nor anything else, but a base ruffian. He was the seventh son, and his parents called him Doctor; it was his name, and not the title of his profession.

He once belonged to the Methodist Church, and was excluded for immoralities. He afterwards imposed himself on the Church of Latter Day Saints, and was excluded for using obscene language to a young lady, a member of the said Church, who resented his insult

---

[k]This is incorrect. Rigdon was pastor of the First Baptist Church at Pittsburgh beginning January, 1822. Patterson and Lambdin remained in the printing business until January 1, 1823. See Chapter 4.

[l]Robert Patterson did leave a statement (see page 66 of this book) and said, in part, not only that Spalding had brought his manuscript to Patterson's office, but also that it was written "chiefly in the style of our English translation of the Bible. . . ."

with indignation, which became both her character and profession.[m]

After his exclusion he swore—for he was vilely profane—that he would have revenge, and commenced his work. He soon found assistance; a pious old Deacon of the Campbellite Church, by the name of Ouis Clapp, and his two sons, Thomas J. Clapp and Matthew S. Clapp, both Campbellite preachers, abetted and assisted by another Campbellite preacher, by the name of Adamson Bentley.[n] Hulbert went to work catering lies for the company. Before Hulbert got through, his conduct became so scandalous that the company utterly refused to let his name go out with the lies he had collected, and he and his associates had made, and they substituted the name of E. D. Howe.[o] The change, however, was not much better. There were scandalous immoralities about the Howe family of so black a character that they had nothing to lose, and became good tools for this holy company to work with. A man of character would never have put his name to a work which Hulbert was concerned in.[p] The tale in your paper is one hatched up by this gang before the time of their expulsion.

It has always been a source of no ordinary satisfaction to me to know that my enemies have no better weapon to use against me, or the cause in which I am engaged, than lies; for, if they had any better, they would certainly use them. I must confess, however, that there is some consistency in our persecutors; for, as truth can never destroy truth, it would be in vain for our persecutors to use truth against us, for this would only

---

[m]Joseph Smith offended Rigdon's daughter at a later date, causing quite a scandal.

[n]Rigdon worked with some of these men, since he had been a Campbellite himself.

[o]Howe, an editor, was the author of the well-documented book *Mormonism Unvailed*.

[p]Howe was well-respected. He also wrote a book on the War of 1812, which was widely read, and he was also the editor of *The Painesville Telegraph*.

build us up; this they seem to know, and lay hold of the only available means they have, which are lies. And this, indeed, is the only weapon which can be, or ever has been used against the truth. As our persecutors are endeavoring to stop the progress of truth, I must confess that they act with a degree of consistency in the choice of means, namely, lies; but, if truth would do it, they would surely not have recourse to lies.

In order to give character to their lies, they dress them up with a great deal of piety; for a pious lie, you know, has a great deal more influence with an ignorant people than a profane one. Hence their lies came signed by the pious wife of a pious deceased priest. However, his last act of piety seems to have been to write a bundle of lies, themselves being witnesses; but then his great piety sanctifies them, and lies become holy things in the hands of such excessive piety, particularly when they are graced with a few Reverends; but the days have gone by when people are to be deceived by these false glossings of Reverend's sanctions; the intelligent part of the communities of all parts of the country, know that Reverends are not more notorious for truth than their neighbors.

The only reason why I am assailed by lies is, that my opposers dare not venture on argument, knowing that if they do they fall. They try, therefore, to keep the public from investigating, by publishing and circulating falsehoods. This I consider a high encomium on both myself and the cause I defend.

Respectfully,
S. Rigdon[10]

Rigdon appears to have been overly vehement in his denial of the charges by Mrs. Davison. Specifically, he used the word "lie" in one form or another a total of 19 times in this one rebuttal! Rigdon's credibility would have been greatly improved if he had addressed himself directly to the specific charges stated by Mrs. Davison instead of producing what is, in reality, nothing more than an emotional argument lacking concrete evidence (see Appendix 3).

McKinstry's Rebuttal

We may use this exchange between Rigdon and Mrs. Davison to show the extent of the controversy in the early days of Mormonism. The Spalding theory was not something newly contrived in the twentieth century, but was a volatile issue from the very beginning of Mormonism. By way of rebuttal, let us allow Mrs. Davison's daughter to reply to Rigdon as our investigation of the Conneaut period closes.

Washington, D.C., April 3rd, 1880.

So much has been published that is erroneous concerning the "Manuscript Found," written by my father, the Rev. Solomon Spaulding, and its supposed connection with the book, called the Mormon Bible, I have willingly consented to make the following statement regarding it, repeating all that I remember personally of this manuscript, and all that is of importance which my mother related to me in connection with it, at the same time affirming that I am in tolerable health and vigor, and that my memory, in common with elderly people, is clearer in regard to the events of my earlier years, rather than those of my maturer life.

During the war of 1812, I was residing with my parents in a little town in Ohio called Conneaut. I was then in my sixth year. My father was in business there, and I remember his iron foundry and the men he had at work, but that he remained at home most of the time and was reading and writing a great deal. He frequently wrote little stories, which he read to me. There were some round mounds of earth near our house which greatly interested him, and he said a tree on the top of one of them was a thousand years old. He set some of his men to work digging into one of these mounds, and I vividly remember how excited he

became when he heard that they had exhumed some
human bones, portions of gigantic skeletons, and various relics. He talked with my mother of these dis-
coveries in the mound, and was writing every day as
the work progressed. Afterward he read the manuscript which I had seen him writing, to the neighbors
and to a clergyman,[q] a friend of his, who came to see
him. Some of the names that he mentioned while reading to these people I have never forgotten. They are as
fresh to me today as though I heard them yesterday.
They were Mormon, Maroni, Lamenite, Nephi. We
removed from Conneaut to Pittsburgh while I was still
very young, but every circumstance of this removal is
distinct in my memory. In that city my father had an
intimate friend named Patterson,[r] and I frequently
visited Mr. Patterson's library with him, and heard my
father talk about books with him. In 1816 my father
died at Amity, Pennsylvania, and directly after his
death my mother and myself went to visit at the residence of my mother's brother William H. Sabine, at
Onondaga Valley, Onondaga County, New York. Mr.
Sabine was a lawyer of distinction and wealth, and
greatly respected. We carried all our personal effects
with us, and one of these was an old trunk, in which
my mother had placed all my father's writings which
had been preserved. I perfectly remember the appearance of this trunk, and of looking at its contents. There
were sermons and other papers,[s] and I saw a manuscript, about an inch thick, closely written, tied with
some of the stories my father had written for me, one
of which he called, "The Frogs of Wyndham." On the
outside of this manuscript were written the words,
"Manuscript Found." I did not read it, but looked
through it and had it in my hands many times, and saw

---

[q]Probably Joseph Badger.

[r]This Patterson could have been either Robert or Joseph, since both
men owned the book and printing establishment.

[s]Perhaps Spalding's first novel, *Manuscript Story*, was among these
(see *New Light on Mormonism*, p. 20).

the names I had heard at Conneaut, when my father read it to his friends. I was about eleven years of age at this time.

After we had been at my uncle's for some time, my mother left me there and went to her father's house at Pomfret, Connecticut, but did not take her furniture nor the old trunk of manuscripts with her. In 1820 she married Mr. Davison, of Hartwicks, a village near Cooperstown, New York, and sent for the things she had left at Onondaga Valley, and I remember that the old trunk, with its contents, reached her in safety. In 1828, I was married to Dr. A. McKinstry of Hampden County, Massachusetts, and went there, to reside. Very soon after my mother joined me there, and was with me most of the time until her death in 1844. We heard, not long after she came to live with me—I do not remember just how long—something of Mormonism, and the report that it had been taken from my father's "Manuscript Found";" and then came to us direct an account of the Mormon meeting at Conneaut, Ohio, and that, on one occasion, when the Mormon Bible was read there in public, my father's brother, John Spaulding, Mr. Lake and many other persons who were present, at once recognized its similarity to the "Manuscript Found," which they had heard read years before by my father in the same town. There was a great deal of talk and a great deal published at this time about Mormonism all over the country. I believe it was in 1834 that a man named Hurlburt came to my house at Monson to see my mother, who told us that he had been sent by a committee to procure the "Manuscript Found" written by the Rev. Solomon Spaulding, so as to compare it with the Mormon Bible. He presented a letter to my mother from my uncle, Wm. H. Sabine, of Onondaga Valley, in which he requested her to loan this manuscript to Hurlburt, as he (my uncle) was desirous "to uproot (as he expressed it) this Mormon fraud." Hurlburt represented that he had been a convert to Mormonism, but had given it up, and through the "Manuscript

Found," wished to expose its wickedness. My mother was careful to have me with her in all the conversations she had with Hurlburt, who spent a day at my house. She did not like his appearance and mistrusted his motives, but having great respect for her brother's wishes and opinions, she reluctantly consented to his request. The old trunk, containing the desired "Manuscript Found," she had placed in the care of Mr. Jerome Clark of Hartwicks, when she came to Monson, intending to send for it. On the repeated promise of Hurlburt to return the manuscript to us, she gave him a letter to Mr. Clark to open the trunk and deliver it to him. We afterwards heard that he had received it from Mr. Clark, at Hartwicks, but from that time we have never had it in our possession, and I have no present knowledge of its existence, Hurlburt never returning it or answering letters requesting him to do so. Two years ago, I heard he was still living in Ohio, and with my consent he was asked for the "Manuscript Found." He made no response although we have evidence that he received the letter containing the request. So far I have stated facts within my own knowledge. My mother mentioned many other circumstances to me in connection with this subject which are interesting, of my father's literary tastes, his fine education and peculiar temperament. She stated to me that she had heard the manuscript alluded to read by my father, was familiar with its contents, and she deeply regretted that her husband, as she believed, had innocently been the means of furnishing matter for a religious delusion. She said that my father loaned this "Manuscript Found" to Mr. Patterson, of Pittsburg, and that when he returned it to my father, he said: "Polish it up, finish it, and you will make money out of it." My mother confirmed my remembrances of my father's fondness for history, and told me of his frequent conversations regarding a theory which he had of a prehistoric race which had inhabited this continent, etc., all showing that his mind dwelt on this subject. The "Manuscript Found," she said, was a romance written in Biblical style, and that while she heard it read, she had no special admiration for it more than other romances he wrote and read to her. We never, either of us, ever saw, or in any way communicated with the Mormons, save Hurlburt as above described; and while we have no personal knowledge that the Mormon Bible was taken from the "Manuscript Found," there were many evidences to us that it was and that Hurlburt and the others at the time thought so. A convincing proof to us of this belief was that my uncle, William H. Sabine, had undoubtedly read the manuscript while it was in his house, and his faith that its production would show to the world that the Mormon Bible had been taken from it, or was the same with slight alterations. I have frequently answered questions which have been asked by different persons regarding the "Manuscript Found," but until now have never made a statement at length for publication.

> (Signed)
> M. S. McKinstry.

Sworn and subscribed to before me this 3rd day of April, A.D. 1880, at the city of Washington, D.C.

> Charles Walter, Notary Public.[11]

What was the actual fate of the "Manuscript Found" which was in the possession of Mrs. Davison? Further evidence has convinced us that, in reality, Hurlbut never received the copy of the manuscript from the trunk in Harwick, but that when he traveled there, he and Clark discovered it missing. This would mean that sometime after Mrs. McKinstry's last look at it in either 1827 or 1828 and before Hurlbut's trip in 1834, it was lost. It may have been borrowed by someone else and never returned, with or without Mrs. Davison's permission, or someone in the Clark or even Davison or Sabine family may have neglected to return it to the trunk. As we will show in Appendix 3, both Mrs. Davison and

Mrs. McKinstry were mistaken in thinking that the manuscript was returned by Mr. Patterson. Spalding had a second copy in his own possession in addition to the copy lost at the printshop in Pittsburgh. It was this second copy that Mrs. Davison and Mrs. McKinstry were familiar with.[12]

NOTES

1. Howe, E. D., *History of Mormonism*, pp. 278-80.
2. Ibid., pp. 280-81.
3. Spalding, *The Spalding Memorial*, p. 238.
4. Howe, pp. 282-83.
5. Ibid., pp. 286-87.
6. Ibid., p. 284.
7. Ibid.
8. Ibid., p. 285-86.
9. Spalding, pp. 240-41.
10. Page, *The Spalding Story*, pp. 11-13.
11. *Scribner's Magazine*, "The Book of Mormon," (August, 1880), p. 616.
12. Mrs. E. E. Dickinson wrote the affidavit for Mrs. McKinstry and commented: "I wrote this statement at Mrs. McKinstry's dictation, and was obliged to change it and copy it four times before she was satisfied, so anxious was she that no word or expression should occur in it to which she could not solemnly make oath" (*Scribner's*, p. 616). Mrs. Dickinson described Mrs. McKinstry as "a remarkably intelligent and conscientious woman . . ." (p. 613).

   Mrs. McKinstry's husband and son were both outstanding medical doctors, and her son-in-law, Mr. Seaton, was Chief Clerk in the Census Bureau in Washington, D.C. Note that she states that the names "Mormon, Moroni, Lamanite, Nephi" were ones she never forgot. Those names, she said were familiar to her before she ever heard of Mormonism or *The Book of Mormon*. From 1817 to around 1828 she handled the manuscript "many times" and saw those same names repeatedly!

   In a letter from her to A. B. Deming (1887), Mrs. McKinstry writes, "It [*Manuscript Found*] contained the words, 'Lehi, Lamoni, Nephi. . . .' " In this same letter she also said that she had "often seen" the *Manuscript Found* during the years between 1817 and 1828. There is some testimony to the effect that Mrs. Davison may have seen the man who could have spirited her copy of the manuscript from the trunk. She said, "A man of the name of Smith was, between 1823 and 1827, frequently seen prowling around the house [at Hartwick] without any ostensible object, and so suspicious were his manoeuvres, that he was once or twice arrested as a common vagabond, and only escaped the penalties of the law by running away" (*American Review*, "The Yankee Mahomet," p. 555). Although uncorroborated by known court records or other testimony, Mrs. Davison was sure of her statement. Perhaps it is unrelated to Joseph Smith's activities, but it is interesting to know that Joseph was arrested, tried, and convicted of being a "glass-looker" (fortune-teller) only thirty miles from Hartwick in 1826!

Spalding's Last Years

From 1812 to 1814, Solomon Spalding and his family lived in Pittsburgh, Pennsylvania, and it was during this time that Spalding took his manuscript to the printer. In 1814 the family moved to nearby Amity out of concern for Spalding's health and the general high cost of living in the growing city of Pittsburgh. Here, on October 20, 1816, Solomon Spalding died.

Our previous brief sketch of Spalding's life gives us the outline for this period. He moved to Pittsburgh in hopes of having *Manuscript Found* published and then, from its profits, paying all of his debts. His manuscript was delivered to Patterson's Print Shop. During the long period it lay in the shop, the foreman (Silas Engles) and Mr. Robert Patterson became familiar with the contents. After Spalding moved to Amity, he wrote the long-delayed preface and title page and returned with them to the printers to add to the otherwise-prepared manuscript. Upon his arrival it was discovered that the manuscript was missing, and Spalding then concluded that it had been taken by Sidney Rigdon, who was much later to figure so prominently in the early days of Mormonism.

At Amity, Spalding kept a nonalcoholic "temperance tavern" and often spoke to his friends and guests of his manuscript and even read it aloud to them frequently. His always-poor health finally failed him, and he died penniless and ignorant of the ultimate end to which his manuscript was going to be put.

Of the period just before Spalding's move from Conneaut to Pittsburgh we have a detailed description included in a longer chronicle of Spalding's life. This affidavit was written by Rev. Abner Jackson, whose father was a friend of Spalding in Conneaut and who was himself acquainted with Spalding during that time.

It is a fact well established that the Book called the Book of Mormon, had its origin from a romance that was written by Solomon Spaulding in Conneaut, a small village in Ashtabula County, Ohio, about A.D. 1812. Spaulding was a highly educated man about six feet high, of rather slender build, with a dark complexion, black eyes, black hair, rather slow of speech, never trifling, pleasant in conversation, but seldom laughing aloud. His deportment was grave and dignified in society, and he was much respected by those of his acquaintance. He was a clergyman of the Presbyterian order, and for a time a settled pastor in the city of New York. So said his brother John Spaulding and others in the neighborhood, who heard him preach. It was said that failing health caused him to resign the pastorate. He then came to Richfield, Otsego County, New York, and started a store, near where my father lived, about the beginning of the present century. Spaulding contracted for large tracts of land along the shore of Lake Erie, on each side of the state line, in both Pennsylvania and Ohio. My father exchanged with him, the farm on which he lived in Otsego County, New York, for land in Erie County, Pa., where the town of Albion now stands, and moved on it A.D., 1805. It was then a dense forest. Shortly after my father moved, Spaulding sold his store in Richfield, and moved to Conneaut, Ashtabula County, Ohio, and built a forge on Conneaut Creek, two miles from Conneaut Harbor, and two miles from the state line. In building this he failed, sold out, and about the beginning of the year 1812, commenced to write his famous romance called by him the Manuscript Found.

This romance, Mr. Spaulding brought with him on a visit to my father, a short time before he moved from Conneaut to Pittsburgh. At that time I was confined to the house with a lame knee, and so I was in company with them and heard the conversation that passed between them. Spaulding read much of his manuscript to my father, and in conversation with him, explained his views of the old fortifications in this country, and told his romance. A note in Morse's Geography suggested it as a possibility that our Indians were descendants of the lost tribes of Israel. Said Morse, they might have wandered through Asia up to Behring's Strait, and across the strait to this continent. Besides there were habits and ceremonies among them that resembled some habits and ceremonies among the Israelites of that day. Then the old fortifications and earth mounds, containing so many kinds of relics and human bones, and some of them so large, altogether convinced him that they were a larger race and more enlightened and civilized than are found among the Indians among us at this day. These facts and reflections prompted him to write his Romance, purporting to be a history of the lost tribes of Israel.

He begins with their departure from Palestine, or Judea, then up through Asia, points out their exposures, hardships and sufferings, also their disputes and quarrels, especially when they built their craft for passing over the straits. Then after their landing, he gave an account of their divisions and subdivisions under different leaders but two parties controlled the balance. One of them was called the righteous, worshipers and servants of God. These organized with prophets, priests and teachers, for the education of their children, and settled down to cultivate the soil, and to a life of civilization. The others were idolators. They contended for a life of idleness; in short, a wild, wicked, savage life.

They soon quarreled, and then commenced war anew, and continued to fight, except at very short intervals. Sometimes one party was successful and sometimes the other, until finally a terrible battle was fought, which was conclusive. All the righteous were slain, except one, and he was Chief Prophet and Recorder. He was notified of the defeat in time by Divine authority; told where, when and how to conceal the record, and He would take care that it should be preserved, and brought to light again at the proper time, for the benefit of mankind. So the Recorder professed to do, and then submitted to his fate. I do not remember what that fate was. He was left alone of his party. I do not remember that anything more was said of him.

IN MEMORY OF

Solomon Spaulding, who departed this life Oct. 20th, A.D., 1816. Aged 55 years.

"Kind cherubs guard the sleeping clay,
    Until the great decision day,
    And saints complete in glory rise,
    To share the triumph of the skies."

[Abner Jackson's statement continues],

Spaulding frequently read his manuscript to the neighbors and amused them as he progressed with his work. He wrote it in Bible style. "And it came to pass" occurred so often that some called him "Old Come to Pass."

So much for Spaulding's romance; now for the Book of Mormon. The first account of the Book of Mormon that I saw, was a notice in my father's newspaper, stating that Joseph Smith, Jr., professed having dreamed that an angel had appeared to him and told him to go and search in a place he named in Palmyra, N.Y., and he would find a gold-leaf Bible. Smith was incredulous and did not go until the second or third time he dreamed the same dream. Then he said he went, and, to his surprise, he found the golden Bible, according to his dreams. But it was written in a language so ancient that none could be found able either to read it or tell in what language it was written. Some time after, another statement appeared that an angel had consented to read and interpret it to Joseph Smith, and he should report it to a third person, who should write it in plain English, so that all might read the new Bible and understand its import. Some time after, in 1830, the book was published at Palmyra, N.Y., called a New Revelation; the Book of Mormon. This purports to be a history of the lost tribes of the Children of Israel. It begins with them just where the romance did, and it follows the romance very closely. It is true there are some verbal alterations and additions, enlarging the production somewhat, without changing its main features. The Book of Mormon follows the romance too closely to be a stranger. In both many persons appear having the same name; as, Maroni, Mormon, Nephites, Moroni, Lama, Lamanite, Nephi and others.

Here then we are presented with romance second, called the Book of Mormon, telling the story of the same people, traveling from the same plain, in the same way having the same difficulties and destination, with the same wars, same battles and same results, with thousands upon thousands slain. Then see the Mormon account of the last battle at Cumorah, where all the righteous were slain. They were called the Nephites, the others were called Lamanites (see Moroni's account of the closing scene), "and now it came to pass that a great battle was fought at Cumorah. The Lamanites slew all the Nephites (except Moroni), and he said, I will write and hide up the

Record in the earth, and whither I go, it mattereth not."—Book of Mormon, Page 344, third American Edition.[a] How much this resembles the closing scene in the Manuscript Found. The most singular part of the whole matter is, that it follows the romance so closely, with this difference: the first claims to be a romance; the second claims to be a revelation of God, a new Bible! When it was brought to Conneaut and read there in public, old Esq. Wright heard it, and exclaimed, "Old Come to Pass has come to life again." Here was the place where Spaulding wrote and read his manuscript to the neighbors for their amusement and 'Squire Wright had often heard him read his romance. This was in 1832, sixteen years after Spaulding's death. This 'Squire Wright lived on a farm just outside of the little village. I was acquainted with him for twenty-five years. I lived on his farm when I was a boy and attended school in the village. I am particular to notice these things to show that I had an opportunity of knowing what I am writing about.

After I commenced writing this article, I heard that an article in Scribner's Monthly for August, 1880, on the Book of Mormon, contained a note and affidavit of Mrs. Matilda S. McKinstry, Solomon Spaulding's only child, stating that she remembered her father's romance. I sent at once for the Monthly, and on the 613, 614, 615, and 616 pages, found the article and her testimony. Her statement from the commencement, until they moved to Pittsburgh, in all essential particulars I know to be true. She relates those acts as they occurred to my own personal knowledge, though she was then a little girl. She is now about seventy-five years of age.

I stated before that I knew nothing of Spaulding after he moved to Pittsburgh, except by letters and newspapers. He soon moved to Amity, Washington County, Pa., and shortly after this he died and his wife went to her brother's. His daughter's account of the

---

[a]This is not an exact quotation (C. Shook, p. 109).

deceitful method by which Hurlburt gained possession of and retained Spaulding's manuscript, is, I
think, important and should not be lost sight of. She
was no child then. I think she has done her part well in
the vindication of the truth by her unvarnished statement of what she remembered of her father's
romance. I have not seen her since she was a little girl,
but I have seen both of these productions, heard
Spaulding read much of his romance to my father and
explain his views and reasons for writing it. I also have
seen and read the Book of Mormon, and it follows
Spaulding's romance too closely to be anything else
than a borrowed production from the romance. I think
that Mrs. McKinstry's statement fills a gap in my account from Spaulding's removal to Pittsburgh, to the
death of his wife in 1844. I wish, if my statement is
published that hers also be published with it, that the
truth may be vindicated by the truth beyond any
reasonable doubt.

(Signed)
Abner Jackson
Canton, Ohio, December 20, 1880.[1]

Rev. Jackson's statement is one of the most complete,
lengthy, and well-documented among the many similar
affidavits concerning the Spalding/Rigdon thesis. On the
strength of his testimony alone, the probable truth of the
thesis is truly astounding.

However, coupled with the overwhelming number of
complementary testimonies, and with the conclusive cor-
relations in the intertwining lives of the three princi-
pals—Smith, Rigdon, and Spalding—it would be impossible for an objective observer to believe Rigdon's dis-
claimers.

Rev. Robert Patterson, owner of the Patterson Print
Shop, added his statement to the other accounts. He
declared what he knew of the affair in 1842:

"R. Patterson had in his employment Silas Engles at the time, as a foreman printer, and general superintendent of the printing business. As he, (S.E.) was an excellent scholar, as well as a good printer, to him was entrusted the entire concerns of the office. He even decided on the propriety of otherwise publishing manuscripts when offered—as to their morality, scholarship, &c., &c. In this character he informed R. P. that a gentleman, from the East originally, had put into his hands a manuscript of a singular work, chiefly in the style of our English translation of the Bible, and handed the copy to R. P. who read only a few pages, and finding nothing apparently exceptionable, he (R. P.) said to Engles, he might publish it, if the author furnished the funds for good security. He (the author) failing to comply with the terms, Mr. Engles returned the manuscript, as was supposed at that time, after it had been some weeks in his possession with other manuscripts in the office.

"This communication, written and signed 2d, April, 1842.

"Robert Patterson"[2]

The Reverend Williams who interviewed Rev. Patterson to obtain this statement added, "Mr. Patterson firmly believes, also, from what he has heard of the Mormon Bible that it is the same thing he examined at that time."[3]

Patterson distinctly remembered, it is important to note, that Spalding's manuscript was written ". . .chiefly in the style of our English translation of the Bible. . . ."

The Consistent Testimony of Joseph Miller

In 1814, Spalding moved with his family to Amity, Pennsylvania, not far from Pittsburgh. Pittsburgh had been growing, and with its growth it became a much more expensive city in which to live. Spalding's small income was unable to cope with the rising costs of living there, and so he felt that Amity, a small town, would be more within his means. In addition, Amity's climate was better for his health. Spalding operated a temperance tavern there which proved to be a more stable economic venture than most he had engaged in. He was able to provide adequately for his wife and daughter. However, his health was not significantly improved, and he finally died on October 20, 1816.

Miller lived and worked in Amity during this period and spent many evenings in the Spalding home (tavern), often listening to the retired preacher read his novel. He helped tend Spalding during his last illness and made his coffin.

Throughout the years after the publication of the controversial "Golden Bible," Miller was asked to relate his knowledge of the *Manuscript Found*. An examination of his testimonies in 1869, 1879, and twice in 1882 show that he never changed his convictions about the matter.

In March of 1869 he declared:

> When Mr. Spaulding lived in Amity, Pa., I was well acquainted with him. I was frequently at his house. He kept what is called a tavern. It was understood that he had been a preacher; but his health failed him and he ceased to preach. I never knew him to preach after he came to Amity. He had in his possession some papers which he said he had written. He used to read select portions of these papers to amuse us of evenings.
>
> These papers were detached sheets of foolscap. He said he wrote the papers as a novel. He called it the "Manuscript Found," or "The Lost Manuscript Found." He said he wrote it to pass away the time when he was unwell; and after it was written he thought he would publish it as a novel, as a means to support his family.

Some time since, a copy of the book of Mormon came into my hands. My son read it for me, as I have a nervous shaking of the head that prevents me from reading. I noticed several passages which I recollect having heard Mr. Spaulding read from his "Manuscript." One passage on the 148th page (the copy I have is published by J. O. Wright & Co., New York) I remember distinctly. He speaks of a battle, and says the Amalekites had marked themselves with red on the foreheads to distinguish them from the Nephites. The thought of being marked on the forehead with red was so strange, it fixed itself in my memory. This together with other passages I remember to have heard Mr. Spaulding read from his "Manuscript."

THE SPALDING HOME AND TAVERN
1814-16, Amity, Pennsylvania

Those who knew Mr. Spaulding will soon all be gone, and I among the rest. I write that what I knew may become a matter of history; and that it may prevent people from being led into Mormonism, that most seductive delusion of the devil. From what I know of Mr. Spaulding's "Manuscript" and the book of Mormon, I firmly believe that Joseph Smith, by some means, got possession of Mr. Spaulding's "Manuscript," and possibly made some changes in it and called it the "Book of Mormon."

(Signed)
Joseph Miller, Sr.
March 26, 1869.[4]

AMITY TODAY

Ten years later, in 1879, Miller furnished another statement to Dr. W.W. Sharpe, which was printed in *The Pittsburgh Telegraph* on February 6, 1879.

I was well acquainted with Mr. Spalding while he lived in Amity, Pa. I would say he was from 55 to 60 years of age; in person tall and spare, and considerably stooped, caused in part, I think from a severe rupture. His hair was quite gray. He was chaste in language and dignified in manner, becoming his profession. I never heard him preach, think he never preached at all said he had quit preaching on account of ill health. He kept a public house or tavern of the character common to that day. He died of desentery in 1816 in the Fall, I think after an illness of six or eight weeks. Dr. Cephas Dodd attended him.

I watched with him many nights during this illness. After he died I made his coffin and superintended his burial. One night when near his end, he told me he thought he should die, and requested me to assist his wife in settling his estate; accordingly I, with Col. Thos. Venom went on her bond as administratrix, and I helped her close it up. Mrs. Spaulding was intelligent and of pleasing manners, with fair complexion, and say from 35 to 40 years of age. A child of fair complexion and about fourteen years of age, lived with them there, think she was their daughter as she bore the Spaulding name.

Mr. S. was poor but honest. I endorsed for him twice to borrow money. His house was a place of common resort especially in the evening. I was presenting my trade as a carpenter, in the village and frequented his house. Mr. S. seemed to take delight in reading from his manuscript written on foolscap for the entertainment of his frequent visitors, heard him read most if not all of it, and had frequent conversations with him about it.

Some time ago I had in my possession, for about six months, the book of Mormon, and heard most of it read during that time. I was always forcibly struck with the similarity of the portion of it which purported to be of supernatural origin to the quaint style and peculiar language that had made such a deep impression on my mind when hearing the manuscript read by Mr. S. For instance, the very frequent repetition of the phrase, "and it came to pass." Then on hearing read the account from the book of the battle between the Amalekites and the Nephites, in which the soldiers of one army, had placed a red mark on their foreheads to distinguish them from their enemies, it seemed to reproduce in my mind not only the narrative, but the very words as they had been impressed on my mind by the reading of Spaulding's manuscript.

The Object of Mr. S. in writing the "Manuscript Found," as I understood, was to employ an invalid's lonely imagination, and to support a romantic history of those last races or tribes, whose true history remains buried with their dust beneath those mysterious mounds so common in a large portion of our country.

Its publication seemed to be an after thought most likely suggested by pecuniary embarrassment. My recollection is that Mr. S. had left a transcript of the manuscript with Mr. Patterson, of Pittsburgh, Pa., for publication, that its publication was delayed until Mr. S. would write a preface, and in the meantime the transcript was spirited away and could not be found. Mr. S. told me that Sidney Rigdon had taken it, or that he was suspicioned for it. Recollect distinctly that Rigdon's name was used in that connection.

The longer I live the more firmly I am convinced that Spaulding's MS. was appropriated and largely used in getting up the Book of Mormon. I believe, that leaving out of the book the portion that may be easily recognized as the work of Joe Smith and his accomplices that Solomon Spaulding may be truly said to be its author. I have not a doubt of it.

On January 20, 1882, Miller wrote a letter to Thomas Gregg, answering Gregg's questions about the Spalding/

Rigdon thesis. This letter is shorter than the previous statement, but it is consistent in its contentions and repeats the essentials to which Miller had already attested.

Ten Mile, Washington Co., Pa.,
Jan. 20, 1882.

Dear Sir—In answer to yours, I would state that I was familiar with Solomon Spaulding. I worked in Amity, where he lived, and as the fashion was that day, we all assembled at his house in the evenings (as he kept tavern), and he frequently would read from his manuscript. The work was very odd. The words "Moreover," "And it came to pass," occurred so often that the boys about the village called him "Old Came to Pass." He told me he lived in Ohio when he wrote his manuscript. He said he lost his health, and he commenced writing a history of the mounds near where he lived, or of the people who built them. He afterwards removed to Pittsburgh, and kept a little store to support his family, and while there he took his manuscript to Mr. Patterson, then engaged in a publishing house. Mr. Patterson told him if he would write a title page he would publish it. He left a copy and moved to Amity. He afterwards went back to have his MS. published, but it could not be found. He said there was a man named Sidney Rigdon about the office, and they thought he had stolen it. The passage you refer to, on page 148, as Cooper has it, is in reference to being marked with red in their forehead. "Nephites," I recollect distinctly, as occurring very often; as to "Lamanites" it is not so distinct—and a great many other names that were very odd.

The MS. that I say, would not, I think make as large a book as the Book of Mormon.

Spaulding was a very poor man; during his stay at Amity, I was very familiar with him, bailed him for money at least twice; and by request of Spaulding, assisted his wife some in settling up his little business—made his coffin and helped lay him in his grave.

> (Signed)
> Joseph Miller.[5]

Less than a month later, on February 13, 1882, he wrote another letter to another inquirer on the same subject.

Ten Mile, Pa., Feb. 13, 1882

I rec. yours of the 1st Feb., contents duly noted you state you wish to get all the information in my possession in regard to Solomon Spaulding. I knew the man very well, was intimately acquainted, often heard him read from what he called his MS, he came to our house and wanted me to go with him and bail him for 50 Dollars as he needed the money and while on the road he told some of his history, he said while living in Ohio he lost his health and in looking over the Country where he lived he discovered some mounds, they appeared to be the work of an ancient race of people and he concluded he would write their history or a fictitious novel of the people that built the mounds, after living there, he told me he moved to Pittsburg and while there he applied to Mr. Patterson to have his novel printed for the purpose as he stated to help him take care of his family. Patterson said he, Patterson, would publish it, if he, Spaulding, would write a title page. He told me he kept a little store in Pittsburg, he then moved to Amity, leaving a copy of the manuscript in Patterson's hands, after being at Amity some time he went back to Pittsburg, took his title page he called it the Lost Manuscript Found when he went to Pittsburgh the manuscript could not be found, he said there was or had been a man by the name of Sidney Rigdon had stole it; Spaulding did not die at my house as you have it but died at a house he had rented in Amity and kept as a Public house or tavern, he was a man fully six feet high rather stooped forward a little of sober visage, very reserved in conversation and very candid apparently in all his dealings and I think a very good man, it used to be very common at that day for us to gather in at the Public house in the evenings and often Mr. Spaulding would read from his MS. to entertain us. I had the Book of Mormon in my house for about six months for the purpose of comparing it with my recollection of the "Lost Manuscript Found," and I unhesitatingly say that a great part of the historical part of the Book of Mormon is identical with the MS. and I fully believe that the MS. is the foundation of the whole concern.

> Yours Truly
> (Signed)
> Joseph Miller.
> Ten Mille, Washington Co., Pa.[6]

Miller mentioned Dr. Cephas Dodd as the physician who tended Spalding during his final illness in Amity. Dr. Dodd, far from being silent on the matter, backed up Miller's various statements in a short note he wrote on June 5, 1831, on the flyleaf of his copy of *The Book of Mormon.*

This work, I am convinced by facts related to me by my deceased patient, Solomon Spaulding, has been made from the writings of Spaulding, probably by Sidney Rigdon, who was suspicioned by Spaulding with purloining his manuscript from the publishing-house to which he had taken it; and I am prepared to testify that Spaulding told me that his work was entitled, "The Manuscript Found in the Wilds of Mormon; or Unearthed Records of the Nephites." From his description of its contents, I fully believe that this Book of Mormon is mainly and wickedly copied from it.

> Cephas Dodd
June 5, 1831.[7]

Dr. Dodd knew Spalding and treated him for two years at Amity. He was one of the first "pioneers" in

Amity and was well-respected and trusted by the entire community.

Picture of Dr. Cephas Dodd

Redick McKee

Rev. Redick McKee lived in Amity, Pennsylvania, for over 1½ years during the period the Spaldings lived there. He tended store down the street from the tavern and boarded with Spalding. In April of 1869, in Washington, D.C., he saw Joseph Miller's statement in the paper and offered his unsolicited support for Miller.

Washington, D.C. April 14, '69

Messers. Editors:—Here on business with the Government, I have accidentally found in the Wheeling Intelligencer of the 8th Inst., an article copied from your paper under the caption, "Who wrote the book of Mormon." The statement of Mr. Joseph Miller, Sr., enclosed in the communication of your correspondent, J. W. Hamilton, carries me back in memory, to scenes and occurrences of my youth, at the pleasant old village of Amity, in your county, and are corroborative in some measure, of their conjecture as to the real author of that curious production, the "Mormon Bible."

With a view to throw some additional light upon a subject, which in the future, if not at present, may possess historical importance, I have concluded to employ a leisure hour in giving you some of my recollections, touching the "Lost History found," and its author.

In the tail of 1814 I arrived in the village of "good will," and for 18 or 20 months, sold goods in the store previously excepted by Mr. Thomas Brico. It was on the Main street, a few rods west of Spalding's tavern, where I was a boarder. With both Mr. Solomon Spalding and his wife, I was quite intimately acquainted. He was regarded as an amiable, inoffensive, intelligent old gentleman, of some sixty winters; and as having been formerly a teacher or professor in some eastern Academy or College, but I was not aware of his having been a preacher or called "Reverent." He was afflicted with a rupture, which made locomotion painful, and confined him much to his house. They possessed but little of this world's goods, and as I understood, selected Amity as a residence, because it was a healthy and inexpensive place to live in.

I recollect quite well Mr. Spalding spending much time in writing on sheets of paper torn out of an old book, what purported to be a veritable history of the nations or tribes, who inhabited Canaan when, or before, that country was invaded by the Israelites under Joshua. He described with great particularity, their numbers, customs, modes of life, their wars, strategems, victories, and defeats, &c. His style was flowing and grammatical, though gaunt and abrupt; very like the story of the "Maccabees" and other apochryphal books in the old bibles. He called it "Lost History Found,"—"Lost Manuscript," or some such name; not disguising that it was wholly a work of the imagination, written to amuse himself, and without any immediate view to publication. I read, or heard him read, many wonderful and amusing passages from different parts of his professed historical records; and was struck with the minutences of his details, and the apparent truthfulness and sincerity of the author. Defoe's veritable Robinson Crosoe, was not more reliable! I have an indistinct recollection of the passage referred to by Mr. Miller, about the Amelekites making a cross with red paint on their foreheads to distinguish them from enemies in the confusion of battle, but the manuscript was full of equally ludicrous descriptions. After my removal to Wheeling in 1818, I understood, that Mr. Spalding had died, and his widow had reported to her friends in northern Ohio, or western New York. She would naturally take the manuscript with her. Now it was in northern Ohio, probably in Lake or Ashtabula county, that the first Mormon prophet, or imposter Jo. Smith lived, and published what he called the "Book of Mormon," or the "Mormon Bible."[b] It is quite probable therefore, that with some alterations, the "Book of Mormon" was in fact the "Lost Book," or "Lost

---

[b]Mrs. Spalding moved to western New York, where, we have already shown, Joseph was arrested in 1826, scarcely thirty miles from her residence.

History Found," of my old landlord, Solomon Spalding, of Amity, Washington County, Pennsylvania.

I have also a recollection of reading in some newspaper about the time of my removal to California in
1850, an article on this subject, charging Jo Smith
directly, with perloining, or in some improper way,
getting possession of a certain manuscript, which an
aged clergyman, had written for his own amusement,
as a novel, and out of it making up his pretended
Mormon bible. Smith's converts or followers, were
challenged to deny the statement. Both the date and
name of the paper, I have forgotten. Possibly in your
own file of the Reporter, some notice of the matter
may be found to verify my recollection.

Many changes have occurred in old "Cat Fish's
Camp," as well as in "Amity," since I first knew them,
Mr. Joseph Miller, Sr., as I presume, my old friend, Jo.
Miller, with whom in 1815 I had many a game of
house ball, at the east side of Spalding's tavern. If so,
and this article meets his eye he will recall the stripling
who sold house, nearly opposite good old Tibba
Cook's residence, in Amity. He was then in the prime
of life, always in a good humor; told a story well; a
good shot with a rifle; and the best ball player in the
crowd. When he and I happened to be partners, we
were sure to win. I was with him many happy days in a
green old age. If any of these desultory recollections of
the olden time, can aid in any way the truth of history,
and the suppression of a miserable imposter, use them
as you deem proper, either in print or in the waste
basket.

> Respectfully,
> Redick M'Kee[8]

Another testimony, much more detailed, was made
by McKee in January of 1886. This statement, which is
22 pages long, contains more information concerning
Spalding and his *Manuscript Found* than almost any
other statement concerning this period in Spalding's life.

We found the statement just before this book was to be printed and were pleased to discover that it confirmed many of the ideas we had formulated earlier for which we wanted additional evidence. The original of this statement is in the Chicago Historical Society. We have reproduced below those portions of it which directly pertain to our subject.

I . . . proceeded to Amity, a village ten miles from Washington [Pennsylvania] on the road to Waynesburg in Greene County. It was near the 10-mile Creek, surrounded by rich farming lands, occupied chiefly by a sober and industrious population, mostly from New Jersey. I was introduced by Mr. Chambers to a number of citizens; confirmed the arrangement made for a store-house; then went to the hotel or public-house and was introduced to the landlord who proved to be Mr. Solomon Spaulding. He received us courteously; expressing the hope that I would find the little room a pleasant residence, and that while the store would be a great convenience to the town and neighborhood, it would prove profitable to its owners. There I spent my first night in Amity.

. . . I had frequent calls from the Messrs Chambers, Mr. Spaulding and Ziba Cook Esq; and through them became acquainted with many others, who called from curiosity or to make purchases.

. . . During all of this time I was a boarder in the family of Mr. Spaulding, and became quite intimate with him.

He was afflicted with a serious rupture which prevented him from taking much exercise in the open air, but in good weather he called at the store almost every afternoon. I regarded him as a gentleman of the old school; affable in manners, and very instructive in conversation. He was about six feet in height, with a large frame though much reduced in flesh, and weighing only about 150 pounds. He was well posted in the current news of the day, in Europe as well as our own country. He gave me much interesting information about our late war with Great Britain, its causes and its progress until happily concluded by the treaty of Ghent. He deprecated the cowardly surrender of Detroit by General Hull; applauded the bravery and success of our fleets on the northern lakes, and particularly the brilliant victory of General Jackson at New Orleans. This battle was fought after the treaty had been signed. There were no steamships or telegraph wires at that day to bring the news earlier.

I have since learned that Mr. Spaulding was considered the most learned man in Ashtabula County, Ohio, and that he was both a versatile and a prolific writer. In Amity I know he was a moral man, a strict observer of the Sabbath, and an attendant upon public worship; and I had no cause to doubt his being a true believer. As an evidence of my confidence in his integrity, I invariably left the store in his charge when I was absent a day or two from the village at Washington or elsewhere. . . . When the weather was inclement I occasionally visited him in his room, and almost always found him at his table, reading or writing. One day when I called he was writing upon foolscap paper, taken from some old account book. My curiosity was excited, and I said to him, that if he was writing letters I could furnish him with more suitable paper. He replied that he was not writing letters, but at another time when I had leisure he would tell me more about it. Shortly after this I called again and the conversation about his writing was renewed. First, he told me of his removal from Western New York to Conneaut, Ashtabula County, Ohio, (where his brother John had property and afterwards resided) expecting to engage in some active business. He said that in connection with Mr. Henry Lake he built a furnace for the manufacture of iron or iron wares. This proved unprofitable and resulted in a failure, which left him liable for debts to a large amount. After the failure he had much leisure time, he said, which he had employed in examining the Indian mounds that abound in that neighborhood; and it was about them he was writing when I first called. He told me also about his other engagements at this time.

But touching these I will give below his daughter's (Mrs. McKinstry's) recollections, recently narrated by her to me, which I think more full and explanatory than my own. This lady is still residing in Washington, D. C., with the family of her late son-in-law, Col. Seaton of the Census Bureau, in remarkably good health for a lady of her age. She corroborated her father's statement about his removal to Conneaut in 1809, his examining the Indian mounds &c, and distinctly recollected that he wrote two or more stories in support of the theory that the Indians of North America were lineal descendants of the Jews from Palestine. In the first of these he brought the Jews from Palestine to America via Italy during the reign of Constantine, and set forth that at Rome they engaged shipping to convey them to some place in Great Britain, but encountered stormy weather and were finally wrecked somewhere on the coast of New England. What became of the manuscript of this story she did not know with certainty but understood that it was published in some Eastern review or magazine.

This romance he afterwards abandoned and set about writing a more probable story founded on the history of the ten lost tribes of Israel. She thought her father must have had wonderful powers of imagination and memory, great command of language and facility of description. Many of his descriptions were of a historical and religious character. Others were grotesque and ludicrous in the extreme.

She remembered that in one of them, touching the mode of warfare in that day, (being hand to hand or man with man) he represented one of the parties having streaks of red paint upon their cheeks and foreheads to distinguish them from enemies in battle. This story he called "The Manuscript Found." It purported to give a history of the ten tribes, their disputes and dissensions concerning the religion of their fathers, their division into two parties; one called Nephites the other Lamanites; their bloody wars, followed by reunion and migration via the Red Sea to the Pacific Ocean; their residence for a long time in China; their crossing the ocean by Behrings Straits in North America, thus becoming the progenitors of the Indians who have inhabited or now live on this continent. This was the story which her Uncle John, Mr. Lake, Mr. Miller and other neighbors heard him read at Conneaut on different occasions. They were all much interested in it and advised him strongly to have it published. Such was not his intention at first, but he finally acceded to their advice, in the hope that from its sale he might obtain money to pay, at least, a portion of his indebtedness. He revised it accordingly. Hearing that there was a publishing house in Pittsburgh he made preparations for removing to that city. To effect this he sold his furniture and some of his books, and, further assisted by his brother, made the journey, arriving she thought, early in 1812. She also recollected that he wrote for her own amusement and instruction, a story called: "Frogs of Wyndham", which she retained for some years, but afterwards lost. She reminded me of many incidents that occurred at Amity and afterwards, which had escaped my memory. For the first year or two after arriving at Amity her father seemed to be benefitted in health, but in the last year of his life was occasionally very ill and confined to the house. He was fond of reading and writing; was a strict observer of the Sabbath; was intimate with Dr. Dodd—our minister—and had frequent conversations with him on religious subjects. Both were well acquainted with the Greek language of the New Testament as spoken in the days when our Saviour was on earth. She also remembered Mr. Joseph Miller who lived near the village, as a frequent visitor, who attended her father in his last illness and was with him at his death; very kindly superintending his funeral and afterwards assisted her mother in settling up the business preparatory to their return to Western New York.

Mr. Spaulding told me that at Pittsburg he became acquainted with the Rev. Robert Patterson who, then in advanced life, was keeping a bookstore with a publishing department attached. He had prepared a copy of his manuscript for the printer and left it with Mr. Patterson for examination. About its publication they had frequent conversation. Mr. P. thought favorably of the printing, but his manager of the publishing department—a Mr. Engles or English—had doubts about its being remunerative and thought the author should either deposit some money to pay the expenses, or, at least, give security for their payment. This was a damper, as he was unable at the time to meet either of the requirements, and the manuscript was laid aside in the office for further consultation. About this time he was informed by a friend that Amity was a healthy and inexpensive place to live in; that a public-house there would shortly be vacated and be for rent at a moderate rate. After consideration and further inquiry he concluded to remove his family to that village, and did remove in October 1814, rented the hotel and opened it, as a public-house, but without a bar. Mr. Spaulding told me that while at Pittsburg he frequently met a young man named Sidney Rigdon at Mr. Patterson's bookstore and printing-office, and concluded that he was at least an occasional employee. He was said to be a good English and Latin scholar and was studying Hebrew and Greek with a view to a professorship in some college. He had read parts of the manuscript and expressed the opinion that it would sell readily. While the question of printing was in abeyance Mr. S. wrote to Mr. P. that if the document was not already in the hands of the printer he wished it to be sent out to him in order that he might amend it by the addition of a chapter on the discovery of valuable relics in a mound recently opened near Conneaut. In reply Mr. P. wrote him that the manuscript could not then be found, but that further search would be made for it. This excited Mr. Spaulding's suspicions that Rigdon had taken it home. . . .

. . . It was during my residence in Virginia and on the Pacific Coast, (many years after I left Amity) that

Mormonism was invented and had its growth, but until my return to the East in 1867, I paid little or no attention to the subject, and for some time considered it a harmless delusion, like other heresies which have sprung up, had their day, and passed away. Seeing in the newspapers frequent reference to the names of Solomon Spaulding, Sidney Rigdon and Joseph Miller revived my recollections of early life at Amity, my intimate acquaintance with Mr. Spaulding and Mr. Miller, and what the former told me about his having written in Ohio a romance or historical novel called "The Manuscript Found", his suspicions about Rigdon &c. I was thus led to examine the publications made at that time, particularly, a work written by Prof. Turner, letters of Mrs. Davidson—formerly Mrs. Spaulding—and by Mrs. McKinstry—her daughter— the testimony of John Spaulding, Henry Lake and others, all tending to prove that the Mormon Bible was a fraud and imposture, not a second revelation of the Will of God, as claimed, but taken from or founded upon a romance or novel written by Solomon Spaulding. . . . In 1869 I wrote to the editor [of The Washington Reporter] that Mr. Miller was an old friend of mine at Amity in 1815-16, and corroborated his statement in relation to what Mr. Spaulding told him about his book, his suspicions of Sidney Rigdon &c; for, I had heard from Mr. S. myself, many of the same things. I wrote also to Mr. Patterson at Pittsburg to the same effect. . . . I was driven in the carriage by J. F. Miller to the residence of his father— my old friend, Joseph Miller—on the road to Amity. I found Mr. Miller to be in remarkably good health for a man in his 88th year (some eight or nine years my senior), and spent the evening and most of the next day in pleasant conversation about our intercourse and occurrences at Amity 64 years before. He had read the Book of Mormon carefully and was convinced that it was founded substantially upon the work written by Mr. Spaulding in Ohio. He was a particular friend of Mr. Spaulding, who died in October 1816—a month or two after I had left the village. . . . Mr. Miller had been a ruling elder in the Cumberland Presbyterian Church for over forty years, and what is remarkable, three of his sons were also ruling elders, one in Pennsylvania, one in Ohio and one in Indiana. . . . I mention this that you may judge of the character and credibility of Mr. Miller as a witness.

This statement of McKee is valuable in that it not only gives a more detailed rendition of his own knowledge of Spalding and his novels, but also records the testimonies of Joseph Miller and Spalding's daughter. His death notice testifies to his remarkable intellect and memory: "He retained to the last the use of his mental powers and his interest in the affairs of Church and State."

TOMBSTONE OF SOLOMON SPALDING

Redfield's Statement

Another boarder adds to our history. Mrs. Ann Treadwell Redfield boarded with the Sabines during the time Mrs. Spalding lived there with her daughter after Spalding's death. Mrs. Redfield was teaching at the time, and as late as 1880 remembered her stay in Onandaga Valley very clearly.

> Syracuse, June 17, 1880
>
> In the year 1818 I was principal of the Onandaga Valley Academy, and resided in the house of William H. Sabine, Esq. I remember the family talk of a manuscript in her possession, which her husband, the Rev. Mr. Spaulding, had written somewhere in the West. I did not read the manuscript, but its substance was so often mentioned, and the peculiarity of the story, that years afterward, when the Mormon Bible was published, I procured a copy, and at once recognized the resemblance between it and Mrs. Spaulding's account of "The Manuscript Found." I remember also to have heard Mr. Sabine talk of the romance, and that he and Mrs. Spaulding said it had been written in the leisure hours of an invalid, who read it to his neighbors for their amusement.
>
> Mrs. Spaulding believed that Sidney Rogdon had copied the manuscript while it was in Patterson's printing office, in Pittsburgh. She spoke of it with regret. I never saw her after her marriage to Mr. Davison of Hartwick (1820).
>
> (Signed)
> Ann Treadwell Redfield[9]

Consistent with the previous testimony, Mrs. Redfield's statement supports the thesis that *The Book of Mormon* is actually a revised edition of Spalding's second novel, *Manuscript Found*. Sabine was a very well-educated man and would hardly have considered the first novel, *Manuscript Story*, "a wonderful story, both in style and substance."[10] Dickinson's book also records

Mrs. Redfield's remembrance, after seeing the Mormon Bible, of the same names and incidents she heard discussed in the Sabine household. Long before Mormonism began in 1830, Mrs. Redfield remembered Mrs. Spalding's belief that Sidney Rigdon had copied or somehow obtained her husband's novel.

Now a plausible scenario can readily be presented which provides Rigdon with the opportunity, motive, and proximity to Spalding's manuscript in order to appropriate it and use it via Smith to found a new religion. In the next chapter we will explore the evidence concerning Ridgon's acquisition of the manuscript, its transmission to Smith, and its eventual emergence as *The Book of Mormon.*[11]

NOTES

1. *Washington Reporter*, January 7, 1881 (originally a letter written to the Historical Society of Washington County, Pennsylvania), as found in *The True Origin of the Book of Mormon*, by Charles Shook, pp. 105-10.
2. Williams, *Mormonism Exposed*, p. 16. Mr. Patterson pastored three churches at different times and had an excellent educational background, having graduated from the University of Pennsylvania in 1791. He taught at the University for four years and managed the Pittsburgh Academy from 1807 to 1810. He and his brother, Joseph, sold and published books and manufactured paper until 1836.
3. Ibid.
4. Creigh, *History of Washington County, Pa.*, pp. 89-93.
5. Shook, pp. 103-4.
6. Dickinson, pp. 240-41.
7. Creigh, p. 429.
8. *The Washington Reporter*, "Solomon Spalding Again," April 21, 1869. Mr. McKee also wrote Robert Patterson from Washington, D.C., on April 15, 1879, and said, "There can be no doubt that the Book of Mormon was founded on and largely copied from the rigorous romance of Solomon Spalding"

(Patterson, Jr., "Solomon Spalding and the Book of Mormon," *History of Washington County, Pennsylvania*), p. 429.

9. Dickinson, pp. 241-42.

10. Ibid.

11. The following are just some of the ingredients in Spalding's life that enhance the probability that a manuscript such as what we now know of as *The Book of Mormon* could have been written by him.

   1. Due to his health, Spalding had sufficient time to write an epic of the proportions of *The Book of Mormon*.

   2. Spalding was fond of writing and spent much of his time writing.

   3. Spalding was in the habit of reading continually and thus was well-enough read to know the major elements used in the manuscript.

   4. Spalding's eccentricity and lively imagination were well-known.

   5. Being deeply in debt, Spalding needed to publish a novel of sufficient interest to sell a large number. The origin of the American Indian was of great public interest at that time.

   6. Spalding's high educational background prepared him for the immense writing task before him.

   7. Being a minister, Spalding knew the Bible well and could easily use it to the advantage of his novel.

   8. *The Book of Mormon* claims to be a historical account of the people of this continent and includes many details of custom, art, science, etc., that were precisely the areas Spalding spent his leisure in reading.

   9. Spalding's experience in the Revolutionary War equipped him to vividly describe all aspects of war and battles such as are seen in *The Book of Mormon*.

10. First Nephi 13:23-32 in *The Book of Mormon* teaches that certain parts of the Bible had been altered or omitted through the centuries, which was a belief held by Spalding.

11. Alma 46:40 teaches that climate and herbs affect one's health to a great extent. This is echoed in Spalding's lifelong parallel beliefs, which led him to move to Amity because of its climate and to ask his physician, Dr. Dodd, for herbs for his illnesses. James Adair's book *The History of the American Indians* teaches the same ideas on this and other subjects found in *The Book of Mormon*. Since it was an extremely popular book on the subject, Spalding probably read it and utilized some of its ideas.

12. Spalding's intense dislike for Masonry is understandable in

the light of the many anti-Masonic publications of his time and earlier. See Ether 8:18-26 and Hela 6:25 (*Book of Mormon*) for two allusions to Masonic-type activities.

13. Several negative references to lawyers, courts, and judges in *The Book of Mormon* (see, for example, Alma 10:13-32) may be explained, if Spalding were the original author, by his disappointment in the legal profession evidenced by his early abandoning of it for theological studies and the ministry.

Spalding to Rigdon: The Manuscript Journey

Sidney Rigdon was born in Library, Pennsylvania, on February 19, 1793. His education was nothing out of the ordinary, but early in life he showed a remarkable interest in history. When Rigdon was seventeen, his father died. Before his father's death, the young boy had fallen from a horse and seriously injured his head. Robert Patterson, in his *Solomon Spalding and the Book of Mormon, History of Washington County, Pennsylvania* (p. 436), quotes from A. H. Dunlevy, who related in 1875 what he had heard of the consequences of the fall from Sidney's brother, Dr. L. Rigdon.

> Sidney Rigdon, when quite a boy, living with his father some fifteen miles south of Pittsburgh on a farm, was thrown from his horse, his foot entangled in a stirrup and dragged some distance before relieved. In this accident he received such a contusion of the brain as ever after seriously to affect his character and

in some respects his conduct. In fact, his brother always considered Sidney a little deranged in his mind by that accident. His mental powers did not seem to be impaired, but the equilibrium in his intellectual exertions seemed thereby to have been sadly affected. He still manifested great mental activity and power, but he was to an equal degree inclined to run into wild and visionary views on almost every question. Hence he was a fit subject for any new movement in the religious world.

Rigdon's Career

As his father before him, Rigdon spent his early life on the farm and did some farming of his own. However, it was thought that he felt farming was somehow beneath his dignity (according to his neighbor, Isaac King) and he left the occupation quickly.

Drawn to city life, Rigdon, then nineteen, traveled to Pittsburgh and stayed there intermittently for the next four years (1812-16). He might have been suited for work in a leather tanner's shop—at least the employment ads of the period show that tanners and tanner's apprentices were in high demand. During this period, he became close friends with J.H. Lambdin, who coincidentally worked as a printer at R. and J. Patterson's Print Shop, the same shop to which Spalding had brought his manuscript. Between 1812 and 1814, the time Spalding lived in Pittsburgh, Spalding brought his manuscript to the shop and left it there, and then, in 1814, moved to Amity, still leaving a copy of the manuscript in the shop. Remembering Rigdon's love of history and his "visionary" tendencies, it is easy to see how Rigdon could have become enthralled with Spalding's story, which he could certainly have encountered through Lambdin.

After Spalding moved to Amity, his manuscript disappeared from Patterson's Print Shop. Spalding told

Dr. Dodd and Rev. Joseph Miller that he suspected Rigdon of the theft.

Spalding died in 1816, and the following year Rigdon was accepted into the membership of the First Baptist Church near his hometown of Library. According to Patterson, his conversion was contrived.[2] He was ordained during 1818 or 1819, and in 1820 he married Phoebe Brooks. Two years later, on January 28, 1822, Rigdon became the minister of the First Baptist Church of Pittsburgh, and it was during this time that he showed Spalding's manuscript to Dr. Winter.

Unfortunately, Rigdon's Baptist ministry was short-lived. He was excommunicated on October 11, 1823, for teaching irregular doctrine, and some have said he was very embittered by the action. Circumstantial evidence seems to point to the period immediately following this as the time Sidney Rigdon and Joseph Smith first met.[3]

From the Baptists, Rigdon moved to the Disciples of Christ (Campbellites) and preached for them until shortly before he was "converted" to Mormonism in 1830. There is conclusive testimony showing that Rigdon possessed Spalding's manuscript until this period, that Rigdon knew Joseph Smith, and that through numerous visits to New York he gave the contents of the manuscript to Smith and his friends, who made some modifications to the text and subsequently published it as *The Book of Mormon*.

Perhaps Rigdon delivered the manuscript to Smith on September 22, 1827, and was the "angel" whom Smith later said gave him the plates! Oliver Cowdery baptized Rigdon into the Mormon Church on November 14, 1830, just seven months after the founding of the church, in Kirtland, Ohio. Rigdon traveled with Edward Partridge to Fayette, New York, where he quickly formed a deep friendship with Joseph Smith. In January, 1831, he and

Smith returned to Kirtland, and Rigdon was established as a leader in the church there.

As a member of the First Presidency of the Mormon Church, Rigdon worked for the Mormons in Ohio, Missouri, and Illinois. Discouraged and disgruntled by strife with the church, Rigdon and his family left the Mormons and moved back to Pittsburgh, where the drama had first begun. On July 14, 1876, Rigdon died in Friendship, New York, having refused to speak concerning the Spalding issue, proclaiming that his "lips were forever sealed on that subject."

The Manuscript Connection

Josiah Spalding, Solomon Spalding's brother, stated, ". . .she [Solomon Spalding's widow] informed me that soon after they arrived at Pittsburgh a man followed them. I do not recollect his name but he was afterwards known to be a leading Mormon. He got into the employment of a printer[a] and he told the printer about my brother's composition."

Mrs. Spalding (Davison) herself stated:

Sidney Rigdon . . . was at that time (1812-14) connected with the printing office of Mr. Patterson, as is well known in that region, and as Rigdon himself has frequently stated. Here he had ample opportunity to become acquainted with Mr. Spalding's manuscript, and to copy it if he chose. It was a matter of notoriety and interest to all who were concerned with the printing establishment.[5]

Solomon Spalding's daughter confirmed Josiah Spalding's testimony in corroborating her mother's convictions on the matter. She declared that her mother

---

[a]Rigdon was not employed at the printshop, but often was seen there with Lambdin.

held a "firm conviction that Sidney Rigdon had copied the manuscript, which had been in Patterson's office in Pittsburgh."[6] We can see from this testimony that, at least to her family, Mrs. Davison maintained the same account concerning Rigdon that she had first proposed before 1820—or *ten years* before *The Book of Mormon* was published and Rigdon joined the new church.

Mrs. A. Treadwell Redfield remembered the early assertions of Spalding's widow and stated, "In the year 1818 I was principal of the Onondaga Valley Academy.... Mrs. Spalding believed that Sidney Rigdon had copied the manuscript while it was in Patterson's printing office, in Pittsburgh. She spoke of it with regret. I never saw her after her marriage."[7] Mrs. Davison was married in 1820, and therefore Mrs. Redfield remembered her testimony from *before* that date and long before Rigdon became a Mormon.

So far we have examined the testimony of family members and acquaintances of Spalding concerning Rigdon's part in the affair. Mormons have raised the challenge that these witnesses might have been somewhat biased and that their testimony might not be as valid as that of a disinterested party. However, the following disinterested party substantiates the claims already set forth by the Spalding family. Mrs. William Eichbaum worked in the Pittsburgh post office during the time Rigdon and Spalding were there, and her testimony is invaluable in determining the true course of events:

My father, John Johnson, was postmaster at Pittsburg for about eighteen years, from 1804 to 1822. My husband, William Eichbaum, succeeded him, and was postmaster for about eleven years, from 1822 to 1833. I was born August 25, 1792, and when I became old enough, I assisted my father in attending to the post-office, and became familiar with his duties. From 1811 to 1816, I was the regular clerk in the office, assorting, making up, dispatching, opening and distributing the mails. Pittsburg was then a small town, and I was well acquainted with all the stated visitors at the office who called regularly for their mails. So meager at that time were the mails that I could generally tell without looking whether or not there was anything for such persons, though I would usually look in order to satisfy them. I was married in 1815, and the next year my connection with the office ceased, except during the absences of my husband. I knew and distinctly remember Robert and Joseph Patterson, J Harrison Lambdin, Silas Engles, and Sidney Rigdon, I remember Rev. Mr. Spaulding, but simply as one who occasionally called to inquire for letters. I remember there was an evident intimacy between Lambdin and Rigdon. They very often came to the office together. I particularly remember that they would thus come during the hour on Sabbath afternoon when the office was required to be open, and I remember feeling sure that Rev. Mr. Patterson knew nothing of this, or he would have put a stop to it. I do not know what position, if any, Rigdon filled in Pattersons's store or printing office, but am well assured he was frequently, if not constantly, there for a large part of the time when I was clerk in the postoffice. I recall Mr. Engles saying that "Rigdon was always hanging around the printing office." He was connected with the tannery before he became a preacher, though he may have continued the business whilst preaching.[8]

Lambdin was a printer in Patterson's shop and was several years younger than Rigdon. While it might be somewhat unusual for a strong friendship to be formed between two people of different ages, it was evidently the case here, and also later, when Rigdon and Smith (who was twelve years Rigdon's junior) became fast friends.

Could Mrs. Eichbaum have confused her statements and actually have been speaking of Rigdon's later stay in Pittsburgh (1822-23)? This is not likely, especially since she linked Spalding with the same period, and he left Pittsburgh in 1814 (and died in 1816). In addition, she dates the period to the time she was the clerk, which was between 1811 and 1816. This reputable eyewitness clearly places Rigdon in Pittsburgh, with Lambdin from Patterson's Print Shop, at the same time Spalding left his novel with the printer.

Attorney R. Patterson (son of R. Patterson, co-owner of the printshop) questioned Mrs. Eichbaum carefully concerning her testimony and concluded that she had "...a memory marvelously tenacious of even the minutest incidents ... and that she had a ... clear mind." He also wrote "... that one who could hear her relate the incidents of her youth, and specify her reasons for fixing names and dates with unusual distinctness, would find it difficult to resist a conviction of the accuracy of her memory."[9]

Answerable Objections

From time to time others have tried to deny Rigdon's presence in Pittsburgh during the time Spalding lived there and the time his manuscript was in the printshop. There are three statements that at first glance seem to refute our theory that Rigdon was indeed in Pittsburgh before 1816.

The first statement was by Peter Boyer, Rigdon's brother-in-law. Only a synopsis of it is available today, taken from the *History of Washington County, Pennsylvania*, by R. Patterson. Patterson says:

Rigdon's relatives at Library, Pa., Carvil Rigdon (his brother) and Peter Boyer (his brother-in-law), in a written statement dated Jan. 27, 1843, certify to the facts and dates as above stated in regard to his birth, schooling, uniting with the church, licensure, ordination, and settlement in Pittsburgh in 1822. Mr. Boyer also in a personal interview with the present writer in 1879 positively affirmed that Rigdon had never lived in Pittsburgh previous to 1822, adding that "they were boys together and he ought to know." Mr. Boyer had for a short time embraced Mormonism but became convinced that it was a delusion and returned to his membership in the Baptist Church.

However, Boyer says that Rigdon never *lived* in Pittsburgh before 1822. What we are asserting is that Rigdon *traveled* periodically to Pittsburgh during the period that Spalding was living there. (Library was situated less than ten miles from Pittsburgh, and therefore travel between the two places was frequent and normal.)

A second testimony raised by Patterson (page 431) was by Samuel Cooper:

Samuel Cooper, of Saltsburgh, Pa., a veteran of three wars, in a letter to the present writer, dated June 14, 1879, stated as follows: "I was acquainted with Mr. Lambdin, was often in the printing-office; was acquainted with Silas Engles, the foreman of the printing-office; he never mentioned Sidney Rigdon's name to me, so I am satisfied he was never engaged there as a printer. I was introduced to Sidney Rigdon in 1843; he stated to me that he was a Mormon preacher or lecturer; I was acquainted with him during 1843-45; never knew him before, and never knew him as a printer; never saw him in the book-store or printing-office; your father's office was in the celebrated Molly Murphy's Row."

It is impossible to determine from this that Rigdon was not in Pittsburgh at the time Spalding was there, since Cooper neglected to state when he himself was in Pittsburgh. It could well have been after 1816—in other words, after Rigdon took Spalding's manuscript and left Pittsburgh for the first time. In this case neither Lambdin nor Engles would have had any reason to mention Rigdon's name to Cooper.

Rev. Robert DuBois was employed by Patterson from 1818 to 1820:

> Rev. Robert P. Du Bois, of New London, Pa., under date of Jan. 9, 1879, writes: "I entered the book-store of R. Patterson and Lambdin in March, 1818, when about twelve years old, and remained there until the summer of 1820. The firm had under its control the book-store on Fourth Street, a book bindery, a printing office (not newspaper, but job office, under the name of Butler and Lambdin), entrance on Diamond Alley, and a steam papermill on the Allegheny (under the name of R. and J. Patterson). I knew nothing of Spalding (then dead) or of his book, or of Sidney Rigdon."

As was the case with Cooper, we find that Du Bois' testimony, as printed by Patterson (pages 431-32), is useless. Du Bois came to Pittsburgh after Rigdon's first tenure, and he left again before Rigdon's residence in Pittsburgh beginning in 1822. It is hardly surprising, then, that Du Bois heard nothing of Rigdon or Spalding.

Finally, Patterson printed the statement of Lambdin's widow:

> "I am sorry to say I shall not be able to give you any information relative to the persons you name. They certainly could not have been friends of Mr. Lambdin."

Lambdin's wife could have known who her husband's friends were, but she did not come to Pittsburgh until 1819, a full five years after Rigdon had left Pittsburgh. Therefore, Lambdin would have had no reason to mention Rigdon to his wife.

There is no credible objection to the evidence that Rigdon was in Pittsburgh during the period from 1813-14, when Spalding's manuscript was in the printshop, when Rigdon was seen by Spalding and suspected of taking the manuscript, and when Mrs. Eichbaum saw Rigdon and Lambdin together.

More Witnesses

Rev. Joseph Miller, who lived in Amity during Spalding's time there, and who tended him during his last illness and made his coffin (see Chapter 4, pages 66-74), stated:

> My recollection is that Spalding left a transcript of the manuscript with Patterson for publication. The publication was delayed until Spaulding could write a preface. In the meantime the manuscript was spirited away, and could not be found. Spaulding told me that Sidney Rigdon had taken it, or was suspected of taking it. I recollect distinctly that Rigdon's name was mentioned in connection with it.[10]

When Miller was carefully questioned he emphatically confirmed that it was Spalding himself who mentioned Rigdon as the culprit, and that he was in no way influenced in his testimony by subsequent events surrounding the rise of Mormonism and Rigdon's prominent position in it.[11]

Miller repeated the essentials of his statement for the book *New Light on Mormonism*, in which he said, "Patterson said he, Patterson, would publish it, if he, Spalding, would write a title page. He told me he kept a little store in Pittsburgh. He then moved to Amity (1814) leaving a copy of the manuscript in Patterson's hands. After being at Amity some time, he went back to Pittsburg, took his title page; he called it the lost manuscript found. When he went to Pittsburg, the manuscript could not be found. He said there was, or had been, a man by the name of Sidney Rigdon had stole it."[12]

Dr. Cephas Dodd was Spalding's physician in Amity (see Chapter 4, pages 74-75) and was by his side at his death in 1816. Dodd early declared his knowledge of the subject, and never once through the years wavered in this testimony concerning Rigdon and Spalding. On June 6, 1831, only a year after the founding of Mormonism, Dr. Dodd received a copy of *The Book of Mormon* and inscribed its flyleaf with the following terse indictment of Rigdon:

> This work I am convinced by facts related to me by my deceased patient, Solomon Spaulding, has been made from writings of Spaulding, probably by Sidney Rigdon, who was suspicioned by Spaulding with purloining his manuscript from the publishing house to which he had taken it; and I am prepared to testify that Spaulding told me that his work was entitled, "The Manuscript Found in the Wilds of Mormon; or Unearthed Records of the Nephites." From his description of its contents, I fully believe that this Book of Mormon is mainly and wickedly copied from it.[13]

At a ceremony in honor of Spalding in 1905, Dr. Dodd's son Elias (1823-1908) told the crowd present there essentially the same thing, remarking that his father had told him this is what had happened.[14]

George French, whose wife was related to Rigdon, confirmed that in 1832 Dr. Dodd accompanied him to Spalding's grave in Amity and declared that Rigdon was the person who had taken the manuscript and converted it into *The Book of Mormon*.[15]

Rev. R. McKee, who had boarded with the Spaldings in Amity (see Chapter 4, pages 75-85) adds to our testimony, although his statement seems to reflect that he was not very knowledgeable about this specific event, even though he was well-versed on other areas of Spalding's life, as shown in his other testimony. He declared:

> Mr. Spaulding told me that he had submitted the work to Mr. Patterson for publication, but for some reason it

was not printed, and afterwards returned to him. I also understood he was then occasionally re-writing, correcting, and he thought improving some passages descriptive of his supposed battles. In this connection he spoke of the man Rigdon as an employee in the printing or book-binding establishment of Patterson and Lambdin, in Pittsburgh; but about him I made no special inquiries.[16]

In an interview with A.B. Deming, in Washington, D.C., McKee reiterated his previous testimony, stating that

> . . . he kept store in Amity, Pa., for a Pittsburgh firm, and that he boarded with Solomon Spaulding and heard him tell about his "Manuscript Found," and that he did not read a copy that was in the house because there was a corrected copy at Patterson's Printing Office in Pittsburgh, Pa., and he intended to purchase a copy when published. [Deming continues] . . . Rigdon obtained possession, I know not how, of the corrected copy Patterson had. It is not improbable that Spaulding rewrote the "Manuscript Found" several times; it was such an original and strange work.[17]

Rigdon's acquaintances also testified about the Spalding/Rigdon episode. Consider the statement of Dr. J. C. Bennett, who was intimately acquainted with both Smith and Rigdon during the Mormon tenure in Nauvoo, Illinois. In 1842 he quarreled with Smith and quickly issued the following testimony:

> I will remark here . . . that the Book of Mormon was originally written by the Rev. Solomon Spaulding, A.M., as a romance, and entitled the "Manuscript Found," and placed by him in the printing-office of Patterson and Lambdin, in the city of Pittsburgh, from whence it was taken by a conspicuous Mormon divine, and re-modeled, by adding the religious portion, placed by him in Smith's possession, and then published to the world as the testimony exemplifies. This I

have from the Confederation,[b] and of its perfect correctness there is not a shadow of a doubt. There never were any plates of the Book of Mormon, excepting what were seen by the spiritual, and not the natural, eyes of the witnesses. The story of the plates is all chimerical.[18]

Mormons have often attacked the testimony of John C. Bennett, since he left the Mormons after disagreeing with Joseph Smith. However, Parly Pratt, the wife of an early Mormon leader, testified to the veracity of Bennett's statements:

> Salt Lake City
> March 31/86

> This certifies that I was well acquainted with the Mormon Leaders and Church in general, and know that the principle statements in John C. Bennetts book on Mormonism are true.
> Sarah M. Pratt

---

[b]The inner circle of Smith's friends.

As we previously stated, Rigdon left the Church of Jesus Christ of Latter Day Saints in 1844. At that time he spoke to James Jeffries while both he and Jeffries were in St. Louis. Jeffries relates the incident:

> Forty years ago I was in business in St. Louis. The Mormons then had their temple in Nauvoo. I had business transactions with them. I knew Sidney Rigdon. He told me several times that there was in the printing office with which he was connected, in Ohio, a manuscript of the Rev. Spaulding, tracing the origin of the Indians from the lost tribes of Israel. This M.S. was in the office several years. He was familiar with it. Spaulding wanted it published, but had not the means to pay for the printing. He [Rigdon] and Joe Smith used to look over the M.S. and read it on Sundays. Rigdon said Smith took the MS. and said, "I'll print it," and went off to Palmyra, New York.[19]

Although Jeffries mislocated the printshop in Ohio (since both Rigdon and Spalding had each previously lived in Ohio), his testimony agrees in substance with the previous statements. At the time of this statement (1884) Jeffries was living in Maryland and dictated his words to Rev. Calvin D. Wilson in the presence of his wife and Dr. J.M. Finney.

A brief statement has come down through the years to us from Judge W. Lang, who was Oliver Cowdery's law partner in Tiffin, Ohio (Cowdery was one of the witnesses to *The Book of Mormon* and its chief scribe). Lang related that "Rigdon got the original ("Ms. Found") at the job printing office in Pittsburg. . . ."

Finally, another founding Mormon, Martin Harris, revealed the true source of *The Book of Mormon* to R. W. Alderman in 1852 (Harris was one of the three witnesses to *The Book of Mormon* but had by this time left the church). Harris and Alderman were snowbound in a hotel in Mentor, Ohio, and shared some conversation while waiting for the weather to clear. Alderman remembered, "Rigdon had stolen a manuscript from a printing office in Pittsburgh, Pa., which Spalding, who had written it in the early part of the century, had left to be printed, but the printer refused to print it, but Jo [Smith] and Rigdon did, as the Book of Mormon."[20]

Rigdon was a Baptist minister for just over three years, until he was excommunicated in October, 1823. During the time he was a Baptist minister, there was some talk by him of Spalding's manuscript being in his possession. Our only witness of this time who has left us a record of Rigdon's assertions is Dr. J. Winter, who was an acquaintance of Rigdon's. History has left us one of Dr. Winter's own statements and two supporting statements concerning him, one by his stepson and one by his daughter. Dr. Winter declared:

> A Presbyterian minister, Spalding, whose health had failed, brought this to the printers to see if it would pay to publish it. It is a romance of the Bible.

Rigdon reportedly said the above words to Winter while both men were looking at the manuscript in Rigdon's church office in Pittsburgh. Rev. A. G. Kirk stated that in 1870-71 Dr. Winter repeated the same statement to him in New Brighton, Pennsylvania.[19]

Dr. Winter's stepson, Rev. Bonsall, remembered his father's comments about Rigdon and Mormonism, and that his father had seen the manuscript. He said, "Rigdon had shown him [Winter] the Spalding manuscript romance, purporting to be the history of the American Indians, which manuscript he [Rigdon] had received from the printers."[21]

Mrs. Mary W. Irvine, Winter's daughter, remembered just what her stepbrother had remembered concerning the affair. She was adamant in her remembrance that her father had *frequently* repeated his sentiments.

> I have frequently heard my father [Dr. Winter] speak of Rigdon having Spaulding's manuscript, and that he had gotten it from the printers to read it as a curiosity; as such he showed it to my father; and that at that time Rigdon had no intention of making the use of it that he afterwards did; for father always said Rigdon helped Smith in his scheme by revising and making the Mormon Bible out of Rev. Spaulding's manuscript.[22]

A.B. Deming solicited her testimony for his book, *Naked Truths about Mormonism*, and Mrs. Irvine replied with the following letter:

> Mr. A. B. Deming—Sir: Your letter of November 1 received two days since. My father left no papers on the subject, but I distinctly recollect his saying that Sidney Rigdon showed him the Spaulding Manuscript as a literary curiosity left in the office to be published if it was thought it would pay. When father saw the "Book of Mormon" he said it was Rigdon's work, or he had a hand in it; I do not remember his words entirely, so many years have elapsed, but that was the import.
>   Respectfully,
>   Mary W. Irvine[23]

Planning a New Religion

From the specific testimony concerning Spaulding's manuscript and Rigdon's possession of it, we move now to the activities of Sidney Rigdon during the time when we believe he became acquainted with Joseph Smith and the two formulated their new religion.

The testimony of his contemporaries leads us to believe that Rigdon not only desired a new religion that was more in line with his visionary ideas, but that the religion he was looking for was what came to be known as Mormonism. Contemporaries testify that he hinted at many of the Mormon doctrines as much as two years before he was "converted" to Mormonism; that he was frequently engrossed in a manuscript that had great future religious implications; and that Mormonism itself was well-known to him long before he officially joined the Mormon Church and before he was ever supposed to have heard of it.

In 1826-27 Rigdon was living in Bainbridge, Ohio. During this time he was seen reading a manuscript and engaged in writing and studying. We think he was preparing Spalding's novel for its debut as the Mormon Bible.

Mrs. Amos Dunlap was the niece of Rigdon's wife. She remembered the manuscript which her uncle possessed from when she was a small child:

> When I was quite a child I visited Mr. Rigdon's family (1826-1827). He married my aunt. They at the time lived in Bainbridge, Ohio. During my visit Mr. Rigdon went to his bedroom and took from a trunk which he kept locked a certain manuscript. He came out into the other room and seated himself by the fireplace and commenced reading it. His wife at that moment came into the room and exclaimed, "What! you're studying that thing again?" Or something to that effect. She then added, "I mean to burn that paper." He said, "No, indeed, you will not. This will be a great thing some day." Whenever he was reading this he was so completely occupied that he seemed entirely unconscious of anything passing around him.[24]

Rigdon had by this time left the Baptist Church and had become a preacher for the Disciples of Christ (Campbellites). He was always known to be a flowery speaker, and his sermons were often punctuated with emotional utterances concerning the coming great religious truths. He did not confine himself to preaching in Disciple churches, but would espouse his views in almost any church or congregation that would have him. In the period of 1826-27, Rigdon was living in Bainbridge, Ohio, and in addition to the above testimony of his niece, there were other testimonies from that period from his acquaintances—contemporaries that together build a framework around the picture of Rigdon as a manuscript purloiner. Harvey Baldwin, of Aurora (Portage County), Ohio, was the son of one of the members of a Baptist church in which Rigdon preached at that time. Baldwin declared that his father heard Rigdon preach in the church in Bainbridge and visited Rigdon's home several times. When he would arrive at the Rigdon home, he would often find Rigdon in a room by himself, and each time Rigdon would hurriedly put away books and papers he was examining, as if he did not wish them to be seen.

Deacon Clapp, of the same Baptist church in Bainbridge, said that he was eighteen when Rigdon came to Mentor, and that he often saw Rigdon's large chair where he spent much of his time writing. The chair had a leaf on one arm on which to write and a lockable drawer underneath. The chair was covered with ink spots, and Rigdon told Clapp that "he had much use for it.[25]

New Doctrines?

The Book of Mormon has several striking teachings, among which is its clear teaching about holding possessions in common, a situation frequent among the characters of Spalding's epic. Stephen H. Hart stated:

> I came to Mentor, O., in 1826 and have since resided here. I was well acquainted with Sydney Rigdon and other Mormon leaders. . . . I attended Rigdon's preach-

ing and heard him urge the church to put their property in the common fund and have all things common. I have heard Mrs. Mann and other members of Rigdon's church say that weeks before he joined the Mormons, he took the Bible and slapped it down on the desk and said that in a short time it would be of no more account than an old almanac; that there was to be a new Bible, a new Revelation, which would entirely do away with this. It caused the church to distrust him and but few followed him into Mormonism.[26]

Rev. S.F. Whitney not only corroborated the testimony of Hart, but also expanded on it. He declared:

I was born in Fairfield, Herkimer County, N.Y., March 17, 1804. I saw the Battle of Platsburgh on Lake Champlain; it lasted two hours and forty minutes. I followed boating as hand and captain on the lakes and ocean. I was soundly converted at eighteen on Grand Island, and united with the Methodists. I came to Kirtland, O., in 1826, where my brother, N. K. Whitney kept store. I heard Sydney Rigdon preach in Squire Sawyers' orchard in 1827 or '28. He said how desirable it would be to know who built the forts and mounds about the country. Soon it would all be revealed. He undoubtedly referred to the "Book of Mormon" which was published in 1830. Revival meetings were held in Kirtland in 1827 or '28, by Rigdon, in which he preached orthodox Baptist doctrine on the work of the Holy Spirit. In Mentor he preached against it.[27]

Rev. Darwin Atwater was a zealot for the gospel in his youth and was not afraid to take anyone, preacher or layman, to task if he thought someone was neglecting the fundamentals of the Bible. R. Patterson interviewed Atwater and declared him to be ". . . noted for his strict regard for truth and justice. . . ."

Atwater declared that Rigdon hinted about a book to

be published that would answer all of the questions concerning the history of the inhabitants of the Americas—precisely what *The Book of Mormon* "revealed" just months later. Atwater's statement gives us a great deal of information concerning this period.

> Soon after this, the great Mormon defection came on us [Disciples of Christ]. Sidney Rigdon preached for us, and notwithstanding his extravagantly wild freaks, he was held in high repute by many. For a few months before his professed conversion to Mormonism, it was noticed that his wild, extravagant propensities had been more marked. That he knew before of the coming of the Book of Mormon is to me certain, from what he said on the first of his visits at my father's, some years before. He gave a wonderful description of the mounds and other antiquities found in some parts of America, and said that they must have been made by the Aborigines. He said there was a book to be published containing an account of those things. He spoke of these in his eloquent, enthusiastic style, as being a thing most extraordinary. Though a youth then, I took him to task for expending so much enthusiasm on such a subject, instead of things of the gospel.[28]

As a Campbellite preacher, Rigdon associated with other such preachers during the period under consideration. One preacher he spoke with concerning the "plates" and their story was Rev. Adamson Bentley. One conversation between the two men took place in the presence of Alexander Campbell, the founder of the Churches of Christ (Campbellites). History has preserved for us, fortunately, both Rev. Bentley and Rev. Campbell's statements. Bentley said:

> You request that I should give you all the information I am in possession of respecting Mormonism. I know that Sidney Rigdon told me there was a book coming out (the manuscript of which had been found

engraved on gold plates) as much as two years before
the Mormon book made its appearance in this country
or had been heard of by me. The same I communicated to brother A. Campbell. The Mormon book has
nothing of baptism for the remission of sins in it; and
of course at the time Rigdon got Solomon Spaulding's
manuscript he did not understand the scriptures on
that subject. I cannot say he learnt it from me, as he
had been about a week with you in Nelson and
Windham, before he came to my house. I, however,
returned with him to Mentor. He stated to me that he
did not feel himself capable of introducing the subject
in Mentor, and would not return without me if he had
to stay two weeks with us to induce me to go. This is
about all I can say. I have no doubt but the account in
Mormonism Unmasked [Unveiled] is about the truth.
It was got up to deceive the people and obtain their
property, and was a wicked contrivance with Sidney
Rigdon and Joseph Smith, Jr. May God have mercy on
the wicked men, and may they repent of this their
wickedness!

    May the Lord bless you, brother Scott, and
family!

Yours most affectionately,
Adamson Bentley.[29]

Campbell's statement agrees with Bentley's in every
particular except that Campbell placed the conversation
one year earlier than did Bentley (but still at least three
or four years before Rigdon is supposed to have first
heard about Mormonism). Here is Campbell's statement:

The conversation alluded to in Brother Bentley's letter
of 1841, was in my presence as well as his, and my
recollection of it led me, some two or three years ago,
to interrogate Brother Bentley touching his recollection of it, which accorded with mine in every particular, except the year in which it occurred, he placing
it in the summer of 1827, I in the summer of 1826,

Rigdon at the same time observing that in the plates dug up in New York, there was an account, not only of the aborigines of this country, but also it was stated that the Christian religion had been preached in this country during the first century, just as we were preaching it in the Western Reserve.[30]

John Rudolph, along with his brother, heard Rigdon's sermons consistently for two years before Rigdon joined the Mormon Church. Rudolph remembered well Rigdon's allusions during that time to the coming great religion:

For two years before the Book of Mormon appeared Rigdon's sermons were full of declarations and prophecies that the age of miracles would be restored and more complete revelations, than those in the Bible would be given. When the Book of Mormon appeared all who heard him were satisfied that he referred to it.[31]

In line with Hart's testimony (previously presented) concerning some of Rigdon's "pre-Mormonism" teachings (which were remarkably consistent with the later teachings of *The Book of Mormon*) are the following three statements. It is quite evident from the mass of this testimony that Rigdon was, in a sense, preparing his listeners for the religion to come—Mormonism. First, Dr. S. Rosa, a prominent physician in the state of Ohio, comments on Rigdon's repeated references to the coming new religion:

In the early part of the year 1830, when the Book of Mormon appeared, either in May or June, I was in company with Sidney Rigdon, and rode with him on horseback a few miles. Our conversation was principally upon the subject of religion, as he was at that time a very popular preacher of the denomination calling themselves "Disciples," or Campbellites. He remarked to me that it was time for a new religion to spring up; that mankind were all rife and ready for it. I thought he alluded to the Campbellite doctrine. He said it would not be long before something would make its appearance; he also said that he thought of leaving Pennsylvania, and should be absent for some months. I asked him how long. He said it would depend upon circumstances. I began to think a little strange of his remarks, as he was a minister of the gospel. I left Ohio that fall and went to the state of New York to visit my friends who lived in Waterloo, not far from the mine of golden Bibles. In November I was informed that my old neighbor, E. Partridge, and the Rev. Sidney Rigdon were in Waterloo, and that they both had become the dupes of Joe Smith's necromancies. It then occurred to me that Rigdon's new religion had made its appearance, and when I became informed of the Spaulding manuscript, I was confirmed in the opinion that Rigdon was at least accessory, if not the principal, in getting up this farce.[32]

Mrs. Eri M. Dille's memories of her father's description of Rigdon were committed to paper, and they present us with a picture of Rigdon, just before he joined Mormonism, as a person having visions and experiences almost of the caliber of those Joseph Smith, Jr., claimed to have.

In the autumn of 1830 Sidney Rigdon held a meeting in the Baptist meeting-house on Euclid Creek. I was sick and did not attend the meeting, but my father repeatedly remarked while it was in progress that he was afraid that Rigdon was about to leave the Disciples for he was continually telling of what marvelous things he had seen in the heavens and of wonderful things about to happen and his talks indicated that he would leave the Disciples.[33]

Almon B. Green gave a more extensive testimony regarding Rigdon's activities and convictions immediately preceding his alliance with Smith. Mormonism's most basic doctrine, that of the apostasy of the church and the need of restoration, was clearly preached by Rigdon the summer *before* he was supposed to have first encountered the "restored gospel." His sermon, recalled by Green, has marked similarities to Smith's first vision:

> In the annual meeting of the Mahoning Association held in Austintown in August, 1830, about two months before Sidney Rigdon's professed conversion to Mormonism, Rigdon preached Saturday afternoon. He had much to say about a full and complete restoration of the ancient gospel. He spoke in his flowing style of what the Disciples had accomplished, but contended that we had not accomplished a complete restoration of the Apostolic Christianity. He contended such restoration must include community of goods—holding all in common stock, and a restoration of the spiritual gifts of the apostolic age. He promised that although we had not come up to the apostolic plan in full yet as we were improving God would soon give us a new and fuller revelation of his will. After the Book of Mormon had been read by many who heard Rigdon on that occasion, they were perfectly satisfied that Rigdon knew all about that book when he preached that discourse. Rigdon's sermon was most thoroughly refuted by Bro. Cambell, which very much offended Rigdon.[34]

Clearly, Rigdon knew more than he was telling, although his sermons and private conversations were telling enough! He knew more than a Campbellite unfamiliar with the Golden Bible should know, who claimed never to have heard of it until the end of 1830. Affidavits show Rigdon already teaching that a new religion was coming, including 1) a history of the people of America, 2) communal living, 3) apostasy and restoration of the gospel, and 4) more and complete revelations, including the return of miracles. This is precisely what *The Book of*

Mormon contained, and precisely what was supposed to have been preached to him for the first time in October of 1830.

Even this moderate amount of information should be more than enough to clearly show Rigdon's connection in *The Book of Mormon*/Spalding saga before his official alliance with the Mormon Church in 1830. However, there is much more information, even more conclusive than that which we have already presented. In the next chapter we will examine the gaps in Rigdon's official itinerary, and we will see how those gaps correspond perfectly with Rigdon's visits to Smith, seen and sworn to by Smith's neighbors and acquaintances.

NOTES

1. Howe, pp. 278-80.
2. Patterson, p. 436.
3. Smith's mother said that at about this time a man attempted a union of the different churches in the area. This could possibly have been Rigdon. See Smith, *Biographical Sketches*, p. 90, and McFarland, *Twentieth Century History of the City of Washington and Washington County (Book of Mormon)*, pp. 187-88.
4. Spalding, *The Spalding Memorial*, p. 238.
5. Shook, p. 81.
6. Dickinson, p. 23.
7. Ibid., pp. 241-42. She was mistaken in thinking Rigdon copied it—he took the printer's copy. See Patterson, p. 433.
8. *The Pittsburgh Mercury*, May 20, 1813, states: "Wanted immediately—A tanner and currier—apply at the office of the *Mercury*." Rigdon may have answered this or a similar ad.
9. Ibid., p. 433.
10. *Pittsburgh Telegraph*, February 6, 1879, p. 1, "The Book of Mormon."
11. Patterson, p. 432.
12. Dickinson, pp. 240-41.
13. Shook, p. 120.
14. Patterson, pp. 432-33.

15. Ibid.
16. Ibid., p. 432.
17. Deming, p. 6.
18. Wyl, *Mormon Portraits*, p. 241.
19. Ibid.
20. Deming, p. 12.
21. Patterson, p. 434.
22. Ibid.
23. Deming, p. 29.
24. Patterson, p. 434.
25. Deming, p. 8.
26. Ibid., p. 50.
27. Ibid., p. 16.
28. Patterson, p. 435.
29. Shook, p. 121-22. Mr. Thomas Clapp, who was a deacon in the Baptist church in which Rigdon often preached, supports Bentley's statement with his own recollections:

> Elder Adamson Bentley told me that as he was one day riding with Sidney Rigdon and conversing upon the Bible, Mr. Rigdon told him that another book of equal authority with the bible, as well authenticated and as ancient, which would give an account of the history of the Indian tribes on this continent, with many other things of great importance to the world, would soon be published. This was before Mormonism was ever heard of in Ohio, and when it appeared, the avidity with which Rigdon received it convinced him that if Rigdon was not the author of it he was at least acquainted with the whole matter some time before it was published to the world.

30. Ibid., p. 122.
31. Braden-Kelly debate, p. 45.
32. Ibid., pp. 123-24.
33. Ibid., p. 46.
34. Ibid., p. 46.

6
A Rigdon-Smith Conspiracy?

Our scenario has unfolded in the preceding pages to show us a picture of Spalding as a struggling, ill novelist who died with his dream of a published novel inscribing his name in history remaining as nothing more than that—a dream. Rigdon has shown himself to be a young visionary—perhaps so dedicated to his own dreams that he thought nothing of appropriating for himself Spalding's dream and modifying it from a novel to a new religion. Both Spalding and Rigdon have had their names inscribed in history. But we believe the evidence shows that while Spalding's name remains that of a would-be novelist, Rigdon's name may well go down as that of a book thief whose misguided actions built an empire on a cracked foundation.

Rigdon's act, supported as we believe by the facts,

was much more important than that of improperly obtaining another man's literary work. Rigdon took Spalding's novel and, history shows, transformed it and claimed more for it than any novel could hope to claim—complete inspiration from God. Perhaps we may never know how much of the picture was planned and executed by Rigdon and how much by Smith or Cowdery or others. The evidence points, however, to Rigdon as the instigator and original "discoverer" of the Mormon Bible, Spalding's *Manuscript Found*.

In this chapter we will examine Rigdon's association with Joseph Smith. Did the two meet, as Mormon sources say, after Rigdon's "conversion" in 1830? Or were they intimate acquaintances long before that time? What evidence do we have for declaring that Rigdon took Spalding's manuscript to Smith and that their collaboration (with others) produced in 1830 *The Book of Mormon* as it was first published? The following chart outlines the events detailed in this chapter which link Sidney Rigdon with Joseph Smith.

RIGDON/SMITH CHRONOLOGY

1823-30	Rigdon is evangelist for Disciples of Christ.
1827 (February)	Rigdon's official itinerary (o.i.) shows a gap which continues through April of 1827.
1827 (March)	During this same gap, Lorenzo Saunders saw Smith and Rigdon together near Smith's home.
1827 (June)	Gap in Rigdon's o.i. Mrs. Eaton's testimony places Smith and Rigdon together.
1827 (October)	Gap in Rigdon's o.i. Lorenzo Saunders' testimony again places Smith and Rigdon together. Sometime during 1827, Abel D. Chase saw Smith and Rigdon together.

1828 (June)	Gap in Rigdon's o.i. Smith records that 116 pages of *The Book of Mormon* is missing (*Doctrine and Covenants*, Section 3). Pomeroy Tucker's testimony declares that Rigdon visited Smith at the time the pages were missing.
1828 (August)	Gap in Rigdon's o.i. For the third time, Lorenzo Saunders places Smith and Rigdon together.
1829 (June/July)	Gap in Rigdon's o.i. David Whitmer (founding Mormon) testifies that Smith and Rigdon were together.
1829 (November/ December)	Lorenzo Saunders again saw Smith and Rigdon together.
1830 (April/June)	Gap in Rigdon's o.i. Mr. Pearne testifies that he often saw Smith and Rigdon together.
1830 (August/ November)	Gap in Rigdon's o.i. Lorenzo Saunders heard Rigdon preach on Mormonism in the *summer* of 1830. Mrs. S. F. Anderick saw Smith and Rigdon together several times "during warm weather." *Doctrine and Covenants* 32-33 commands missionaries to "go west" in October, where they "find" and "convert" Rigdon.
1830 (November)	On the fourteenth, Rigdon is baptized into the Mormon Church by Oliver Cowdery.

The Rigdon/Smith Connection

As is clear from the above chronology, Rigdon was away from his ministerial duties without explanation many times between the years of 1827 and 1830. As a matter of fact, his official itinerary (compiled mostly from Mormon sources), lists no fewer than fifteen gaps from 1827 until his conversion to Mormonism in October of 1830.

These absences were noticed by those he associated with as well as by us. Our research intensified when we discovered that these gaps sometimes paralleled events described in *Doctrine and Covenants* to which a confidant would probably be invited. Since his absences were noticed by us and by his contemporaries, why weren't they noticed and investigated by Rigdon's Mormon biographers? Or, if they were noticed and investigated, why weren't the results made public?

Z. Rudolph (whose brother's testimony is presented on page 112 of Chapter 5) had this to say about Rigdon's frequent absences during this period:

> During the winter previous to the appearance of the Book of Mormon, Rigdon was in the habit of spending weeks away from his home, going no one knew where: and that he often appeared very preoccupied, and would indulge in dreamy, imaginative talks, which puzzled those who listened. When the Book of Mormon appeared and Rigdon joined in the advocacy of the new religion, the suspicion was at once aroused that he was one of the framers of the new doctrines, and probably was not ignorant of the authorship of the Book of Mormon.[1]

Mrs. Sophia Munson also noticed Rigdon's absences. She was living directly across from the Rigdon family at the time in question and, although a young girl, knew Rigdon and his wife well and observed Rigdon's more eccentric practices. She was already living on Mentor Road before Rigdon moved there in 1827, when she was seventeen years old. Her statement concerning the years 1827-30, and in particular Rigdon's conversion to Mormonism, is enlightening:

> My parents settled on Mentor Road, four miles west of Painesville, Ohio, in 1810, when I was six weeks old. I well remember when Elder Rigdon came and lived op-

posite our house in 1827. He was very poor, and when he had much company would send his children to the neighbors to borrow knives, forks, dishes and also for provisions. Father kept his horse and cow gratis.

Rigdon was a very lazy man, he would not make his garden and depended on the church for garden supplies. He would sit around and do nothing. He was away much of the time, and sometimes claimed he had been to Pittsburgh, Pa. I was quilting at his house until 1 o'clock at night the day the four Mormons came to convert Rigdon. I heard some of their conversation in the adjoining room. Orson Hyde boarded at our house and attended a select school, also to Rigdon, who taught some evenings.

My parents joined the Cambellite Church, in Mentor, during Eld. Adamson Bentley's protracted meetings, I think, in 1828. Mrs. Rigdon was an excellent woman, and never complained of their poverty.

> (Signed)
> Mrs. Sophia Munson
> Mentor, Ohio, February, 1885.

The true significance of the gaps in Rigdon's itinerary becomes evident only as we examine 1) their number, 2) their timing (in relation to Smith's activities especially), and 3) the testimonies establishing his early relationship with Smith.

Even to the casual observer, the number of Rigdon's absences from his pastorate is unusual. Added to this is the testimony of his acquaintances that these absences consistently were unexplained—and, as our testimony will show, sometimes the brief explanations were contradictory.

Often an absence in Rigdon's schedule corresponds exactly to a particular event recorded by Smith concerning Mormonism or *The Book of Mormon*. For example, a gap in June of 1828 corresponds exactly to Smith's recording that 116 pages of *The Book of Mormon* were lost at this time by Martin Harris. If Rigdon were in possession of Spalding's manuscript, wouldn't it be logical for him to travel quickly to Smith's residence in New York to either replace the missing pages or authorize some substitution?

Finally, we are faced with consistent testimony from Smith's neighbors and others placing Rigdon and Smith together frequently during the three years before the publication of *The Book of Mormon*. Each testimony corresponds to one of the gaps in Rigdon's itinerary.

CHRONOLOGY OF
ELDER RIGDON'S SCHEDULE

YEAR	MONTH	DAY	EVENT
1826	Nov.	2	Marriage of Smith and Giles.
1826	Dec.	13	Above marriage recorded.
1827	Jan.		Held meeting at Mantua, Ohio.
1827	Feb.		Funeral of Hannah Tanner, Chester, Ohio.
			(Gap of about one month.)
1827	Mar.		Held meeting at Mentor, Ohio.
1827	Apr.		Held meeting at Mentor Ohio.
			(Gap of possibly one month and a half.)
1827	June	5	Marriage of Freeman and Watterman.
1827	June	7	Above marriage recorded.
1827	June	15	Baptized Thomas Clapp at Mentor, Ohio.
1827	July	3	Marriage of Gray and Kerr.
1827	July	12	Above marriage recorded.
1827	July	19	Marriage of Snow and Parker.
1827	Aug.	10	Above marriage recorded.
1827	Aug.	23	Met with Ministerial Assoc., New Lisbon, Ohio.
			(Gap of one month and seventeen days.)
1827	Oct.	9	Marriage of Sherman and Mathews.
1827	Oct.	20	At Ministerial Council, Warren, Ohio.
1827	Oct.	27	Marriage of Sherman and Mathews recorded.
1827	Nov.		Held meeting at New Lisbon, Ohio.

1827	Dec.	6	Marriage of Wait and Gunn.
1827	Dec.	12	Above marriage recorded.
1827	Dec.	13	Marriage of Cottrell and Olds.
1828	Jan.	8	Above marriage recorded.
1828	Feb.	14	Marriage of Herrington and Corning.
1828	Mar.	31	Above marriage recorded.
1828	Mar.		Instructed theological class, Mentor, Ohio.
1828	Apr.		Conducted revival at Kirtland, Ohio.
1828	May		Met Campbell at Shalersville.
1828	June		Baptized H. H. Clapp, Mentor, Ohio.
			(Gap of possibly two months.)
1828	Aug.		At Association, Warren, Ohio.
1828	Sept.	7	Marriage of Dille and Kent.
1828	Sept.	18	Marriage of Corning and Wilson.
1828	Oct.	13	Above marriages recorded.
			(Gap of two months and a half.)
1829	Jan.	1	Marriage of Churchill and Fosdick.
1829	Feb.	1	Marriage of Root and Tuttle.
1829	Feb.	12	Above marriages recorded.
1829	Mar.		Meeting at Mentor, Ohio.
1829	Apr.	12	Meeting at Kirtland, Ohio.
1829	May		Baptized Lyman Wight.
			(Gap of possibly one month and a half.)
1829	July	1	Organized church at Perry, Ohio.
1829	Aug.		Baptized Mrs. Lyman Wight.
1829	Aug.	13	Marriage of Strong and More.
1829	Sept.	14	Above marriage recorded.
1829	Sept.	14	Marriage of Atwater and Clapp.
1829	Sept.		Held meeting at Mentor, Ohio.
1829	Oct.	1	Marriage of Roberts and Bates.
1829	Oct.	7	The last two marriages recorded.
1829	Oct.		At Perry, Ohio.
1829	Nov.		Held meeting at Wait Hill, Ohio.
1829	Dec.	31	Marriage of Chandler and Johnson.
1830	Jan.	12	Above marriage recorded.
			(Gap of possibly two months.)
1830	Mar.		At Mentor, Ohio.
			(Gap of two months.)
1830	June		At Mentor, Ohio.
1830	July		Held meeting at Pleasant Valley, Ohio.
1830	Aug.		Met Campbell at Austintown, Ohio.
			(Gap of easily two-and-a-half months.)
1830	Nov.	4	Marriage of Wood and Cleaveland.
1830	Nov.	11	Above marriage recorded.
1830	Nov.	14	Rigdon baptized by Cowdery.[2]

An examination of the preceding chart shows in detail the activities of Rigdon during this time. Remember, too, that where the record shows "Above marriage recorded," it is not implying that Rigdon was present at the recording. At that time, records were commonly kept by the church secretary, a deacon, or the preacher's wife. Any one of them could and did record the marriages the preacher performed.

The distance between Rigdon's home in Ohio and Joseph's in New York was about 250 miles and could be traveled by horseback in five or six days. A gap in Rigdon's itinerary of even one month would allow ample opportunity for him to have conferred with Smith.

An interesting conjecture concerning the coincidence of Rigdon's activities and Smith's "revelations" concerns the actual production of the manuscript. If Rigdon had actually taken Spalding's manuscript from Patterson's Print Shop in Pittsburgh, surely Silas Engles, foreman of the shop, would have known of Spalding's suspicions concerning Rigdon. Perhaps Engles even knew that Rigdon possessed the story. If Rigdon desired to publish Spalding's *Manuscript Found* as his own work (either as a romance or a revelation), he would certainly do all within his power to see that no one discovered the fraud. For example, he would be much more likely to publish the manuscript after Engles had died.

Is it mere coincidence that Engles died in July of 1827 and that Smith recorded a "revelation" in September of that year, declaring that it was *now* permissible to uncover, translate, and publish the golden plates? This possibility is also supported by the fact that Mrs. Munson remembered that Rigdon had traveled to Pittsburgh at different times—perhaps during the gap in his itinerary the month after Engles' death. This possibility is also supported by the fact that Engles was the last person to link Rigdon conclusively with his close friend, Lambdin, who had died on August 1, 1825.

In 1825 Smith moved to Bainbridge, New York, and was convicted there for "glass-looking," or seeking buried treasure for a fee by means of mystical stones placed in his hat.[3] As previously noted, Bainbridge was only thirty miles from Hartwick, where at the time Spalding's own copy of the manuscript lay at the bottom of his trunk, last seen before Spalding's daughter's marriage in 1828.

All of these conjectures mean nothing, however, if there is no evidence to back them up. We need solid facts to show that Rigdon and Smith were acquainted long before either of them admitted this fact to the public. If Rigdon did make several trips to New York to visit Smith, to prepare him for the office of "prophet" and to give him the Spalding manuscript (including altered portions of it), then one would expect to find that Smith's neighbors knew of Rigdon's visits. We do have that evidence: there are testimonies of eyewitnesses who saw Rigdon and Smith together between 1827 and 1830, before *The Book of Mormon* was published.

The Testimony of Chase

Able D. Chase was a teenager at the time he first saw Rigdon and Smith together, in 1827. He testified:

> Palmyra, Wayne Co., N.Y., May 2, 1879
> I, Abel D. Chase, now living in Palmyra, Wayne Co., N.Y., make the following statement regarding my early acquaintance with Joseph Smith and incidents about the production of the so-called Mormon Bible. I was well acquainted with the Smith family, frequently visiting the Smith boys and they me. I was a youth at the time from twelve to thirteen years old, having

been born Jan. 19, 1814, at Palmyra, N.Y. During some of my visits at the Smiths, I saw a stranger there who they said was Mr. Rigdon. He was at Smith's several times, and it was in the year of 1827 when I first saw him there, as near as I can recollect. Some time after that tales were circulated that young Joe had found or dug from the earth a BOOK OF PLATES which the Smiths called the GOLDEN BIBLE. I don't think Smith had any such plates. He was mysterious in his actions. The PEEPSTONE, in which he was accustomed to look, he got off my elder brother Willard while at work for us digging a well. It was a singular looking stone and young Joe pretended he could discover hidden things in it.

My brother Willard Chase died at Palmyra, N.Y., on March 10, 1871. His affidavit, published in Howe's "History of Mormonism," is genuine. Peter Ingersoll, whose affidavit was published in the same book, is also dead. He moved West years ago and died about two years ago. Ingersoll had the reputation of being a man of his word, and I have no doubt his sworn statement regarding the Smiths and the Mormon Bible is genuine. I was also well acquainted with Thomas P. Baldwin, a lawyer and Notary Public, and Frederick Smith, a lawyer and magistrate, before whom Chase's and Ingersoll's depositions were made, and who were residents of this village at the time and for several years after.

(Signed)
Abel D. Chase

Abel D. Chase signed the above statement in our presence, and he is known to us and the entire community here as a man whose word is always the exact truth and above any possibile suspicion.

Pliny T. Sexton
J. H. Gilbert[4]

In corroboration of our thesis, previously expressed, Chase confirms that Rigdon not only *met* Smith before *The Book of Mormon* was published, but that he was at the Smith's "several times." Sexton, one of the witnesses to Chase's statement, was president of the city bank in Palmyra, and his own word was as trustworthy as that of Chase.

The Testimony of Gilbert and Saunders

Ironically, the second witness, Gilbert, was the proofreader of *The Book of Mormon* at the time of its first printing! However, Gilbert's interest in the Rigdon/Smith relationship was not confined to proofreading. We also have his statement about a conversation he had with Lorenzo Saunders, a resident of Palmyra, who in two separate statements gave us the most complete information on the matter. Gilbert's statement can act as a preface to Saunders' first statement.

Last evening I had about 15 minutes conversation with Mr. Lorenzo Saunders of Reading, Hillsdale Co., Mich. He had been gone about thirty years (from this area). He was born south of our village in 1811, and was a near neighbor of the Smith family—knew them all well; was in the habit of visiting the Smith boys; says he knows that Rigdon was hanging around Smith's for eighteen months prior to the publishing of the Mormon Bible.[5]

SAUNDERS' FIRST STATEMENT
Reading, January 28, 1885
Mister Gregg,
Dear Sir. I received your note ready at hand and will try answer the best I can and give all the information I can as respecting Mormonism and the first origin. As respecting Oliver Cowdery, he came from Kirtland in the summer of 1826 and was about there until fall and took a school in the district where the

Smiths lived and the next summer he was missing and I didn't see him until fall and he came back and took our school in the district where we lived and taught about a week and went to the schoolboard and wanted the board to let him off and they did and he went to Smith and went to writing the Book of Mormon and wrote all winter. The Mormons say it wasn't wrote there but I say it was because I was there. I saw Sidney Rigdon in the Spring of 1827, about the middle of March. I went to Smiths to eat maple sugar, and I saw five or six men standing in a group and there was one among them better dressed than the rest and I asked Harrison Smith who he was and he said his name was Sidney Rigdon, a friend of Joseph's from Pennsylvania. I saw him in the Fall of 1827 on the road between where I lived and Palmyra, with Joseph. I was with a man by the name of Jugegsah, (sp.?). They talked together and when he went on I asked Jugegsah (sp.?) who he was and he said it was Rigdon. Then in the summer of 1828 I saw him at Samuel Lawrence's just before harvest. I was cutting corn for Lawrence and went to dinner and he took dinner with us and when dinner was over they went into another room and I didn't see him again till he came to Palmyra to preach. You want to know how Smith acted about it. The next morning after he claimed to have got plates he came to our house and said he had got the plates and what a struggle he had in getting home with them. Two men tackled him and he fought and knocked them both down and made his escape and secured the plates and had them safe and secure. He showed his thumb where he bruised it in fighting those men. After went from the house, my mother says "What a liar Joseph Smith is; he lies every word he says; I know he lies because he looks so guilty; he can't see out of his eyes; how dare tell such a lie as that." The time he claimed to have taken the plates from the hill was on the 22 day of September, in 1827, and I went on the next Sunday following with five or six other ones and we hunted the side hill by course and could not find no place where the ground had been broke. There was a large hole where the money diggers had dug a year or two before, but no fresh dirt. There never was such a hole; there never was any plates taken out of that hill nor any other hill in that country, was in Wayne county. It is all a lie. No, sir, I never saw the plates nor no one else. He had an old glass box with a tile in it, about 7x8 inches, and that was the gold plates and Martin Harris didn't know a gold plate from a brick at this time. Smith and Rigdon had an intimacy but it was very secret and still and there was a mediator between them and that was Cowdery. The Manuscript was stolen by Rigdon and modelled over by him and then handed over to Cowdery and he copied them and Smith sat behind the curtain and handed them out to Cowdery and as fast as Cowdery copied them, they was handed over to Martin Harris and he took them to Egbert Granden, the one who printed them, and Gilbert set the type. I never knew any of the twelve that claimed to have seen the plates except Martin Harris and the Smiths. I knew all the Smiths, they had not much learning, they was poor scholars. The older ones did adhere to Joseph Smith. He had a peep stone he pretended to see in. He could see all the hidden treasures in the ground and all the stolen property. But that was all a lie, he couldn't see nothing. He was an imposter. I now will close. I don't know as you can read this. If you can, please excuse my bad spelling and mistakes.

Yours With Respect,
From Lorenzo Saunders[6]

Saunders' first statement confirms several possibilities we raised earlier. First, he unequivovably places Rigdon with Smith as early as the spring of 1827. Second, his testimony has clarified Smith's neighbors' opinions of Joseph Smith's character. These opinions fall far short of the opinions presented in most Mormon sources, which portray Smith as a veritable saint throughout all his life. Third, Saunders gave us some tangible information concerning the finding of the "plates." He declared that, in the company of others, he tried to find the hole from which Smith supposedly removed the plates on the hill "Cumorah," but, as much as he searched, there was no hole, no stone, and no lever as Smith had described just the week before.

Saunders' second testimony was given two years after the first and, although shorter, was concise and confirmed his previous testimony in all essentials.

Statement of Lorenzo Saunders.
Hillsdale County, State of Michigan.
Lorenzo Saunders being duly sworn deposes and says:
That I reside in Reading, Hillsdale County, State of Michigan; that I was born in the town of Palmyra, Wayne County, State of New York, on June 7, A.D. 1811, and am now seventy-six years of age. That I lived in said town of Palmyra until I was forty-three of age. That I lived within one mile of Joseph Smith at the time said Joseph Smith claimed that he found the "tablets" on which the "Book of Mormon" was revealed. That I went to the "Hill Comorah" on the Sunday following the date that Joseph Smith claimed he found the plates, it being three miles from my home, and I tried to find the place where the earth had been broken by being dug up, but was unable to find any place where the ground had been disturbed.
    That my father died on the 10th day of October, A.D. 1825. That in March of 1827, on or about the 15th of said month I went to the home of Joseph Smith for the purpose of getting some maple sugar to eat, that when I arrived at the house of said Joseph Smith, I was met at the door by Harrison Smith, Jo's brother. That at a distance of ten or twelve rods from the house there were five men that were engaged in talking, four of whom I knew, the fifth one was better dressed than the rest of those whom I was acquainted with. I inquired of Harrison Smith who the stranger was? He informed me his name was Sidney Rigdon with whom

I afterwards became acquainted with and found to be Sidney Rigdon. This was in March, A.D. 1827, the second spring after the death of my father. I was frequently at the house of Joseph Smith from 1827 to 1830. That I saw Oliver Cowdery writing, I suppose the "Book of Mormon" with books and manuscript laying on the table before him; that I went to school to said Oliver Cowdery and knew him well. That in the summer of 1830, I heard Sydney Rigdon preach a sermon on Mormonism. This was after the "Book of Mormon" had been published, which took about three years from the time that Joseph Smith claimed to have had his revelation.

> (Signed)
> Lorenzo Saunders

Sworn and subscribed to before me this 21st day of July, A.D. 1887.

> (Signed)
> Linus S. Parmelee.
> Justice of the Peace of Reading, Mich.[7]

The most significant statements contained in the above affidavit are: 1) that Lorenzo Saunders could find no evidence of the site where Smith claimed he had dug up the golden plates, even though Saunders searched the hill just the Sunday after Smith claimed his discovery; 2) that the first time Saunders saw Rigdon and Smith together was in March of 1827, *almost 3½ years before Rigdon was supposedly first approached by Mormons*; 3) that Saunders was not only told that the well-dressed stranger was Rigdon, but that Saunders afterwards became personally acquainted with Rigdon; 4) that Cowdery was working on the manuscript *before* Mormon sources say he was (for example, the LDS book *The Restored Church* states on page 35 that Cowdery first met Smith April 5, 1829); 5) that Rigdon preached on Mormonism the summer *before* he allegedly first heard of the "restored gospel"; and 6) that Saunders was qualified to make the above observations, because during the period of time from 1827 to 1830 he was "frequently at the house of Joseph Smith."

The Testimony of Anderick

Another neighbor of the Smiths was Mrs. S.F. Anderick. She was born in 1809, and was two years older than Lorenzo Saunders. She too observed some of the same things as did Saunders. Let her tell her own story.

I was born in New York State near the Massachusetts line, May 7, 1809. In 1812 my parents moved to a farm two miles from the village, and in the township of Palmyra, New York. In 1823 mother died, and I went to her sister's, Mrs. Earl Wilcox, where I lived much of the time until December, 1828, when I went to live with father who had again married and settled on a farm on the Holland Patent, twenty miles west of Rochester, New York. Uncle Earl's farm was four miles south of Palmyra village, and his house was nearly opposite old Jo Smith's, father of the Mormon prophet. Old Jo was dissipated. He and his son Hyrum worked some at coopering. Hyrum was the only son sufficiently educated to teach school. I attended when he taught in the log school house east of uncle's. He also taught in the Stafford District. He and Sophronia were the most respected of the family, who were not much thought of in the community. They cleared the timber from only a small part of their farm, and never paid for the land. They tried to live without work. . . .I have often heard the neighbors say they did not know how the Smiths lived, they earned so little money. The farmers who lived near the Smiths had many sheep and much poultry stolen. They often sent officers to search the premises of the Smiths for stolen property, who usually found the house locked. It was said the creek near the house of the Smiths was lined with the feet and heads of sheep. Uncle's children were all sons, and they played with Smith's younger children, I associated much with Sophronia Smith, the oldest daughter, as she was the only girl near my age who lived in our vicinity. I often accompanied her, Hyrum, and young Jo Smith, who became the Mormon prophet, to apple parings and parties. Jo was pompous, pretentious, and active at parties. He claimed, when a young man, he could tell where lost or hidden things and treasures were buried or located with a forked witch hazel. He deceived many farmers, and induced them to dig nights for chests of gold, when the pick struck the chest, someone usually spoke, and Jo would say the enchantment was broken, and the chest would leave.

Williard Chase, a Methodist who lived about two miles from uncle's, while digging a well, found a gray smooth stone about the size and shape of an egg. Sallie, Williard's sister, also a Methodist, told me several times that young Jo Smith, who became the Mormon prophet, often came to inquire of her where to dig for treasures. She told me she would place the stone in a hat and hold it to her face, and claimed things would be brought to her view. Sallie let me have it several times. but I never could see anything in or through it. I heard that Jo obtained it and called it a peep-stone, which he used in the place of the witch hazel. Uncle refused to let Jo dig on his farm. I have seen many holes where he dug on other farms.

When Jo joined the Presbyterian Church, in Palmyra village, it caused much talk and surprise, as he claimed to receive revelations from the Lord. He also claimed he found some gold plates with characters on them, in a hill between uncle's and father's, which I often crossed. Several times I saw what he claimed were the plates, which were covered with a cloth. They appeared to be six or eight inches square. He frequently carried them with him. I heard they kept them under the brick hearth.

He was from home much summers. Sometimes he said he had been to Broome County, New York, and

Pennsylvania. Several times while I was visiting Sophronia Smith at old Jo's house, she told me that a stranger who I saw there several times in warm weather and several months apart, was Mr. Rigdon. At other times the Smith children told me that Mr. Rigdon was at their house when I did not see him. I did not read much in the "Book of Mormon" because I had no confidence in Jo. Palmyra people claimed that Jo did not know enough to be the author of the "Book of Mormon", and believed that Rigdon was its author. I was acquainted with most of the people about us, and with Martin Harris.

On my way to California I stopped in Salt Lake City from July, 1852, until March, 1853. I received much attention from Mormon ladies because I was acquainted, and had danced with their prophet.

(Signed)

Mrs. S.F. Anderick.

Witnessed by:

Mrs. L.A. Rogers (daughter),

Oscar G. Rogers (grandson).

Subscribed and sworn before F.S. Baker, Notary Public for Monterey County, California, June 24, 1887.[8]

With the introduction of Mrs. Anderick's testimony, more pieces are fitted into the puzzle of Rigdon's early involvement with Smith. Her testimony confirms our thesis that Joseph was a sort of fortune-teller (see Appendix 2), using first witch hazel (probably like a divining rod), and then a stone, which led to his appellation of "peep-stone gazer." Mrs. Anderick also saw what Smith said were the "golden plates" several times. However, as is true with all of the people who "witnessed" the plates, she never actually *saw* them, but only saw something covered with a cloth that Smith *claimed* were the plates!

Mrs. Anderick supplies one piece to our puzzle that none of the previous testimony contained. She declared that Smith was gone often in the summer and had even gone to Pennsylvania. Since Rigdon's travels often took him to Pennsylvania during this time, it is quite conceivable that the two men met several times in Pennsylvania (perhaps in Pittsburgh). Could they have met during the month following the death of Engles, in the summer of 1827?

Mrs. Anderick's testimony provides additional confirmation that Rigdon knew Smith long before 1830, and in fact frequented Smith's house. Mrs. Anderick said that she saw Rigdon "several times in warm weather"; this could hardly refer to Rigdon's public visit in December/January of 1831, because this was certainly not the season of warm weather, and this visit occurred two years after Mrs. Anderick moved to her father's new farm!

The Testimony of Hendrix

A quite detailed statement concerning the origin of *The Book of Mormon* and the relationship between Sidney Rigdon and Joseph Smith was provided by Daniel Hendrix, who as a young man lived in Palmyra and was very well acquainted with Smith and later Rigdon. He said:

> I was a young man in a store in Palmyra, N.Y. from 1822 until 1830 . . . and among the daily visitors at the establishment was Joseph Smith, Jr. Every one knew him as Joe Smith. He had lived in Palmyra a few years previous to my going there from Rochester.
>
> Joe was the most ragged, lazy fellow in the place, and that is saying a good deal. He was about 25 years old. I can see him now, in my mind's eye, with his torn and patched trousers held to his form by a pair of suspenders made out of sheeting, with his calico shirt as dirty and black as the earth, and his uncombed hair

sticking through the holes in his old battered hat. In winter I used to pity him, for his shoes were so old and worn out that he must have suffered in the snow and slush; yet Joe had a jovial, easy, don't-care-way about him that made him a lot of warm friends. He was a good talker, and would have made a fine stump speaker if he had had the training. He was known among the young men I associated with as a romancer of the first water. I never knew so ignorant a man as Joe was to have such a fertile imagination. He never could tell a common occurrence in his daily life without embellishing the story with his imagination; yet I remember that he was grieved one day when old Parson Reed told Joe that he was going to hell for his lying habits.

. . . For over two years Joe Smith's chief occupation was digging for gold at night and sleeping in the daytime. He was close-mouthed on the subject of his gold-seeking operations around on the farms of Wayne County, where not a speck of gold was ever mined and when people joked him too severely concerning his progress in getting the precious metal he would turn his back upon the joker and bystanders and [retreat] as fast as possible. With some of us young men, however, who were always serious with him and affected an interest in his work, he was more confidential.

. . . Finally, in the fall—in September, I believe—of 1828, Joe went about the village of Palmyra telling people of the great bonanza he had at last found. I remember distinctly his sitting on some boxes in the store and telling a knot of men, who did not believe a word they heard, all about his vision and his find. But Joe went into such minute and careful details about the size, weight, and beauty of the carvings on the golden tablets, the strange characters and the ancient adornments, that I confess he made some of the smartest men in Palmyra rub their eyes in wonder. The women were not so skeptical as the men, and several of the leading ones in the place began to feel at once that Joe was a remarkable man after all.

Joe declared, with tears in his eyes and the most earnest expression you can imagine, that he had found the gold plates on a hill six miles south of Palmyra, on the main road between that place and Canandaigua. Joe had dug and dug there for gold for four years, and from that time the hill has been known as Gold Hill.

For the first month or two at least Joe Smith did not say himself that the plates were any new revelation or that they had any religious significance, but simply said that he had found a valuable treasure in the shape of a record of some ancient people which had been inscribed on imperishable gold for preservation. The pretended gold plates were never allowed to be seen, though I have heard Joe's mother say that she had lifted them when covered with a cloth, and they were heavy—so heavy, in fact, that she could scarcely raise them, though she was a robust woman. What Joe at that time expected to accomplish seems difficult to understand, but he soon began to exhibit what he claimed to be copies of the characters engraved on the plates, though the irreverent were disposed to think that he was more indebted to the characters found on China tea chests and in histories of the Egyptians and Babylonians than to any plates he had dug up near Palmyra. Before long, however, a new party appeared on the scene in the person of one Sidney Rigdon, and thenceforward a new aspect was put upon the whole matter.

I remember Rigdon as a man of about 40 years, smooth, sleek, and with some means. He had a wonderful quantity of assurance, and in these days would be a good broker or speculator. He was a man of energy, of contrivance, and would have made a good living anywhere and in any business. He was distrusted by a large part of the people in Palmyra and Canandaigua but had some sincere friends. He and Joe Smith fell in with each other and were cronies for several months. It was after Rigdon and Smith were so intimate that the divine part of the finding of the golden plates began to be spread abroad. It was given out that the plates were a new revelation and were part of the original Bible, while Joe Smith was a true prophet of the Lord, to whom it was given to publish among men.

Rigdon, who from his first appearance, was regarded as the 'brains' of the movement, seemed satisfied to be the power behind the throne. Not only were pretended copies of the engraved plates exhibited, but whole chapters of what were called translations were shown; meetings were held at the Smith house, and in the barns on the adjoining farms which were addressed by Smith and Rigdon, and an active canvass for converts was inaugurated. Strange as it may appear from the absurdity of the claims set forth and the well-known character of Joe Smith, these efforts were to quite a degree successful, particularly among the unsophisticated farmers of the vicinity, and a number of them, who were regarded as equal in intelligence to the average rural population, became enthusiastic proselytes of the new faith.

. . . For three or four years Smith, Rigdon, and Harris worked for converts in the new faith. They all became from constant practice and study good speakers, and Smith was at that time as diligent and earnest as he had previously been lazy and careless. The three men traveled all over New York State, particularly up and down the Erie Canal. Smith would always tell with some effect how the angel had appeared to him, how he felt an irresistible desire to dig where he did, and how he heard celestial music and the chanting of a heavenly host as he drew the golden plates from the earth and bore them to his home.

. . . Of the printing of the 'Book of Mormon' I have a particularly keen recollection. Smith and Rigdon had hard work to get funds together for the new Bible. Smith told me himself that the world was so wicked and perverse that it was hard to win converts: that he had a vision to print the Bible, and that as soon as that was done the work would be prospered wonderfully. . . . The printing office was an upper floor, near the store where I worked, and I was one of the few persons who was allowed about the office while the publishing was going on.

The copy for the Book of Mormon was prepared in a cave that Smith and others dug near the scene of the finding of the golden plates on Gold Hill. I went out there frequently for a Sunday walk during the process of the translation of the plates and the printing of the book. Some one of the converts was constantly about the entrance to the cave, and no one but Smith and Alvin [Oliver] Cowdry, a school teacher there, who had proselytized that season, was allowed to go through the door of the cave. Rigdon had some hopes of converting me, and I was permitted to go near the door, but not so much as to inside.

. . . The publication of the book of 538 pages was pushed with spirit, but until it was completed not a copy was allowed to leave the office. Every volume was packed in the upper room, and the pile they made struck me at the time, and has since been vividly in my mind, as comparing in size and shape with a cord of wood, and I called it a cord of Mormon Bibles. This work was finished in the spring of 1830. Not long after the publication was completed Smith and his followers began their preparations for a removal, and ere long the parties with their converts, packed up all their belongings and left for Kirtland, O.

This removal was not 'on compulsion' from any complaints of their neighbors like those they were subsequently compelled to make from Kirtland and Nauvoo, but all seemed to enter into it readily and with the utmost cheerfulness, though many abandoned homes of great comfort and comparative wealth. In the exodus there were farmers who were customers of the firm where I was employed that sold their farms to the amount of $15,000 all of which was committed to the care and tender mercy of Joe Smith, and the votaries committed themselves to his care and guidance.

Hendrix's testimony was obtained from the Chicago Historical Society and further supports the thesis that Smith and Rigdon were close associates long before Mormonism first reached Kirtland. Hendrix was evidently very well acquainted with both Rigdon and Smith *before* 1831, since Hendrix said he left Palmyra after 1830.

Mormonism Before Mormonism

With the basic fact established that Sidney Rigdon and Joseph Smith were well-acquainted long before Rigdon's official introduction to Mormonism in 1830, we now need to establish the fact that Rigdon was not only in New York, near Smith, during this period, but also that he was preaching Mormonism *before* his "conversion."

K. A. E. Bell lived in Painesville, Ohio, and boarded with a man who was often visited by Rigdon during this period. Bell's testimony lends a great deal of credence to our thesis:

I was born in Harpersfield, Delaware County, New York, December 3, 1803. Our family lived several years in Broome County, N.Y., four miles from Badgers Settlement, where we did our trading. I came to Painesville, Ohio, in 1825, and boarded with Carlos Granger. Whenever Sydney Rigdon, a Baptist minister who lived in Mentor, came to Painesville, he usually stopped with Granger. I have often heard him say at his meals, "How nice it would be to have all Christians live in a community separate from the world's people." After he became a Disciple, he frequently spoke in his sermons of a wondrous light which was soon to burst upon the world. I have heard others say Rigdon, after he became a Mormon, said that Mormonism was the marvelous light he had predicted. I attented the first Mormon meeting Pratt and Cowdery held in Painesville. My brother Milo, from Broome County, N.Y., was present. They told about Prophet Jo Smith finding the gold plates, and said they saw them. My brother ridiculed them after the meeting. He told me he knew Jo Smith when he was digging near the Susquehanna River for Captain Kidd's money. Jo had a peep-stone through which he claimed to see hidden or buried treasures. Jo sold shares to all who would buy, and kept the money. He said they would make a circle, and Jo Smith claimed if they threw any dirt over the circle the money chest would leave. They never found any money. Jo Smith's brother Hyrum's wife was a cousin of Mrs. Bell. It was claimed she died during confinement because her husband refused her the services of a physician. Esek Rosa, an expert accountant and brother of Dr. Rosa, of Painesville, while in conversation with me about Rigdon and Mormonism, several times told me that Rigdon told the people in Mentor and Painesville that he was going to Pittsburgh, Pa., but he went to Rochester, N.Y., instead. Esek said he was visiting in Rochester, and while on the street he was invited to enter a building near by and hear a very smart man preach. Rosa replied, "I think I have heard that voice before." When he entered the room he found Elder Sydney Rigdon preaching Mormonism. This occurred several months before Mormonism was preached in Ohio.

K. A. E. Bell.

Witnessed by: Clara E. Clark

Sworn to and subscribed before me, the undersigned, by K. A. E. Bell, this sixth day of May, 1885. D. Clington Hill, Justice of the Peace, in and for Painesville Township, Lake County, Ohio.[9]

There are four major points to Bell's testimony that have a direct bearing on our thesis. First, Bell confirmed that Rigdon, while he was a Campbellite preacher, taught of a coming "wondrous light" that would be the full restoration of the gospel. In addition, Bell mentioned secondhand information indicating that Rigdon himself declared that Mormonism was the light he was foretelling. Second, the charge of "peep-stone gazer" is further supported by Bell's brother's testimony, reported here, that Smith engaged in that practice repeatedly (without positive results for the investors, but very profitable results for Smith) in Broome County, New York. The third item of interest in the above testimony is the statement, in agreement with our thesis, that Rigdon did not always go where he said he would, but, for example, after saying he was traveling to Pittsburgh he would instead go to Rochester—only a relatively short ride from Palmyra. Finally, Bell's recitation of Rosa's testimony confirms Saunders' testimony that Rigdon was preaching on Mormonism *before* he claimed to have heard of it in Ohio in October/November 1830.

Isaac Butts had an interesting testimony to add to this. He was approximately the same age as Mrs. Anderick and Saunders and remembers the following:

I was born in Palmyra, N.Y., near where old Jo Smith settled, January 4, 1807. I attended school with Prophet Jo. His father taught me how to mow. I worked with old and young Jo at farming. I have frequently seen old Jo drunk. Young Jo had a forked witch hazel rod with which he claimed he could locate buried money or hidden things. Later he had a peep-stone which he put into his hat and looked into. I have seen both. Joshua Stafford, a good citizen, told me that young Jo Smith and himself dug for money in his orchard and elsewhere nights. All the money digging was done nights. I saw the holes in the orchard which were four or five feet square and three or four feet deep. Jo and others dug much about Palmyra and Manchester. I have seen many of the holes. The first thing he claimed to find was gold plates of the "Book of Mormon", which he kept in a pillowcase and would let people lift, but not see. I came to Ohio in 1818, and became acquainted with Sidney Rigdon in 1820. He preached my brother's sermon in Auburn, O., in May 1822. I returned to Palmyra twice and resided there about two years each time. Many persons whom I knew in New York joined the Mormons and came to Kirtland. They told me they saw Sidney Rigdon much with Jo Smith before they became Mormons, but did not know who he was until they came to Kirtland.

(Signed)
Isaac Butts
South Newbury, Geauga Co., O.[10]

Note especially that Butts not only says that Rigdon knew Smith before Mormonism arrived in Ohio, but Butts says that he received this information from people who had *joined* the Mormon Church, and therefore could hardly be called prejudiced against Joseph Smith. He also reiterates that no one was allowed to see the plates, but only to lift the package which Smith *claimed* was the plates.

The statements by W. A. Lillie and Pomeroy Tucker need no comment:

I was born in Trumbull Co., Ohio, in 1815. Our family moved to Chester, the town adjoining Kirtland on the south, in 1822. About 1834 Mr. Pearne, of Chester, told me he used to live in the neighborhood of the Mormon Smith family in Palmyra, N.Y., and was well acquainted with all of them. He said they were a low family and of no account in the community. He told me the summer before Jo Smith, the Mormon prophet, first came to Ohio, he often saw Jo Smith and Rigdon together. It was the first he knew of Rigdon, and it was before the "Book of Mormon" was published. He saw Smith and Rigdon start together in a buggy for Ohio. Mr. Pearne knew Rigdon well after coming to Ohio and said he believed he was at the bottom of Mormonism. My father borrowed the "Book of Mormon" and when he had finished reading it laughed and remarked Rigdon had done pretty well.

W. A. Lillie

Witnessed by:

A. B. Deming

Thomas B. Page.

Sworn to and subscribed in my presence at Willoughby, Lake County, Ohio, this 7th day of March 1885.

A. P. Barber, Justice of the Peace [11]

Here is the statement by Pomeroy Tucker:

A mysterious stranger now appears at Smith's and holds intercourse with the famed money-digger. For a considerable time no intimation of the name or purpose of this stranger transpired to the public, not even to Smith's nearest neighbors. It was observed by some that his visits were frequently repeated. The sequel of the intimacies of this stranger and the money-digger will sufficiently appear hereafter. There was great consternation when the 118 pages of manuscript were stolen from Harris, for it seems to have been impossible, for some unaccountable reason, to retranslate the stolen portion. The reappearance of this mysterious stranger at Smith's at this juncture (1828) was again the subject of inquiry and conjecture by observers, from whom was withheld all explanations of his identity and purpose. When the Book of Mormon appeared, Rigdon was an early convert. Up to this time, he had played his part in the background and his occasional visits to Smith's had been observed by the inhabitants as those of the mysterious stranger. It had been his policy to remain in concealment until all things were in readiness for blowing the trumpet of the new gospel. He now came to the front as the first regular preacher in Palmyra.[12]

Mrs. Eaton, who had lived in Palmyra for 32 years and later interviewed Smith's neighbors concerning Rigdon's association with Smith before 1831, read her findings to the Union Home Missionary Meeting in Buffalo, New York, on May 27, 1881. In part, it said,

> Early in the summer of 1827, a "mysterious stranger" seeks admittance to Joe Smith's cabin. The conferences of the two are most private. This person, whose coming immediately preceded a new departure in the faith, was Sidney Rigdon, a backsliding clergyman, at this time a Campbellite preacher in Mentor, Ohio. [13]

Martin Harris, who financed the launching of the new religion of Mormonism, was not usually disposed to tell of the early beginnings of Mormonism. However, by 1852 he had left the Mormon Church and did discuss what he knew of the Rigdon/Smith affair with R. W. Alderman. Alderman reported the following:

> In February, 1852, I was snowbound in a hotel in Mentor, Ohio, all day. Martin Harris was there, and in conversation told me he saw Jo Smith translate the "Book of Mormon", with his peep-stone in his hat. Oliver Cowdery, who had been a school-teacher, wrote it down. Sidney Rigdon, a renegade preacher, was let in during the translation. Rigdon had stolen a manuscript from a printing office in Pittsburgh, Pa., which Spaulding, who had written it in the early part of the century, had left there to be printed, but the printers refused to publish it, but Jo and Rigdon did, as the "Book of Mormon." Martin said he furnished the means, and Jo promised him a place next to him in the church. When they had got all my property they set me out. He said Jo ought to have been killed before he was; that the Mormons committed all sorts of depredations in the towns about Kirtland. They called

themselves Latter-Day Saints, but he called them
Latter-Day Devils.

> Claridon, Geauga Co., Ohio,
> Dec. 25, 1884
> R. W. Alderman.

Witnessed by:
Clara Alderman,
A. B. Deming.[14]

Since Harris (remembered by Alderman) witnessed
Rigdon there before *The Book of Mormon* was printed, it
must have been before 1830—before Rigdon welcomed
the Mormon missionaries and became a Mormon in
November of 1830!

Finally, the statement of Judge Lang, Oliver
Cowdery's confidant and law partner, provides the final
testimony to substantiate the scene we painted at the
beginning of this chapter. Although he was loyal to his
friend to the end, Lang did feel that he could say the
following concerning what he knew from Cowdery:

> Tiffin, O., Nov. 5, 1881.
>
> Dear Sir:—Your note of the 1st inst. I found upon my
> desk when I returned home this evening and I hasten
> to answer. Once for all I desire to be strictly under-
> stood when I say to you that I cannot violate any con-
> fidence of a friend though he be dead. This I will say
> that Mr. Cowdery never spoke of his connection with
> the Mormons to anybody except me. We were in-
> timate friends. The plates were never translated and
> could not be, were never intended to be. What is
> claimed to be a translation is the "Manuscript
> Found" worked over by C. He was the best scholar
> amongst them. Rigdon got the original at the job
> printing office in Pittsburgh as I have stated.[a] I
> often expressed my objection to the frequent

---

[a]Rigdon did not work there, but was friends with Lambdin, who did.

repetition of "And it came to pass" to Mr. Cowdery and said that a true scholar ought to have avoided that, which only provoked a gentle smile from C. Without going into detail or disclosing a confided word, I say to you that I do know, as well as can now be known, that C. revised the "Manuscript" and Smith and Rigdon approved of it before it became the "Book of Mormon." I have no knowledge of what became of the original. Never heard C. say as to that. . . . I could only answer your questions in the manner I did because some of them were not susceptible of a direct answer by me.

> Resp. Yours,
> W. Lang

Our thesis, on the basis of overwhelming evidence, has traveled from hypothesis to substantiated history. *The Book of Mormon* was not translated from golden plates through miraculous power but was the revised edition of Solomon Spalding's second novel, *Manuscript Found* We are convinced that, based on the evidence, Sidney Rigdon took the manuscript from Patterson's Print Shop, read and revised it for some years until he felt safe in using it, then met Smith and concocted with him the plan of revealing the manuscript as a communication from God. Then Rigdon supervised the work of preparing the manuscript for publication, always keeping closely associated with every move of the young Joseph Smith and his friends.

Much of this evidence has been available before, but to our knowledge it has never before been fully analyzed as integrated evidence which provides a clear look into the actual roots of Mormonism.

However, during the past three years we have uncovered still more evidence that confirms our thesis. We have actually found part of Spalding's novel, in his own handwriting, paralleling *The Book of Mormon* word for word! In the next chapter we will detail this exciting discovery that provides additional proof that novelist Solomon Spalding is the true originator of *The Book of Mormon*.

NOTES

1. Patterson, p. 434.
2. Derived from Shook, pp. 138-44.
3. See Appendix 2.
4. Wyl, p. 231.
5. Ibid., p. 231.
6. Shook, pp. 134-35. Saunders' affidavit ends:

> Charles A. Shook, being duly sworn according to law, deposeth and saith that the foregoing letters of Thomas Gregg and Lorenzo Saunders are verbatim copies (except spelling, punctuation and capitalization) of the originals now in the possession of the American Anti-Mormon Association.
> Charles A. Shook
> Subscribed to in my presence and sworn to before me, at Eddyville, Nebraska, this 13th day of February, 1913.
> B. R. Hedglin, Notary Public.

7. Deming, p. 9.
8. Deming, pp. 9-11. Testimony to the character of Mrs. Anderick is as follows:

> Dear Sir: Mrs. S. F. Anderick, of whom you inquire, is a member of my church. She is a most estimable Christian woman, and is possessed of more than average intellectual ability and culture. She is careful in speech and reliable in judgement; sound in mind and of unimpeachable veracity. Her testimony would be first-class in any court of justice upon any subject with which she might be conversant.
> Respectfully,
> G. W. Izer,
> Pastor Simpson Memorial Methodist
> Episcopal Church,
> San Francisco, Cal.

Dear Sir: I am personally acquainted with Mrs. S. F. Anderick, and have been for two years. She lives on this street, one block from my residence. I have often met her in church, in society, and in her home. I am certain that she is remarkably well preserved, and is sound in mind. She is a woman of intelligence, and of high moral and Christian character.

Always sincerely,
C. H. Fowler,
Bishop of the M. E. Church.

9. Ibid., p. 15.
10. Ibid., p. 11.
11. Ibid., p. 53.
12. Patterson, p. 435. Tucker's conclusions were reached after interviews with Smith's neighbors. Tucker was a proofreader for the original printing of *The Book of Mormon*.
13. Ibid., p. 435.
14. Deming, p. 14.

Manuscript
Found!

The fate of Spalding's original manuscript has been hidden for roughly 150 years. Many theories as to its final destiny have been raised, some by Mormon sources and some by other researchers. Most people who believed the Spalding/Rigdon thesis had little hope of ever seeing Spalding's original manuscript in his own handwriting, since they reasonably assumed that those early Mormons who knew the true origin of *The Book of Mormon* would hardly allow the original manuscript to survive as the ultimate witness against their sacred book. Also, several Mormon arguments have been raised against the Spalding/Rigdon thesis, some of which we will answer in this chapter.

The Quest for Further Knowledge

Yet there was still the hope that somehow the original Spalding manuscript, or a portion of it, would yet be discovered. Walter Martin, one of America's most knowledgeable comparative religion professors, investigated the roots of Mormonism 25 years ago and was convinced by much of the same evidence already presented in this book that Spalding was the original source of *The Book of Mormon*. Since Martin's specialty was religions having their origin in the United States, he spent an unusual amount of time researching the roots of Mormonism. Nothing he uncovered persuaded him that he was wrong in his findings, but in spite of his long hours of study in this matter, he finally had to move to another area of study and to leave some of the pieces of the Mormon puzzle missing. It was always his contention that if someone had the necessary time and determination, all of the missing pieces would be found, including all or part of Spalding's original manuscript. Martin's conviction has been publicly stated in all of his books that deal with Mormonism (see especially *The Kingdom of the Cults*), and it was his conviction that first aroused our interest in the Spalding/Rigdon thesis and solidified our determination to find the missing pieces of the whole picture.

Through hard and tedious work we have uncovered the information presented in the preceding six chapters of this book and in the appendixes. In the early part of 1976 we still did not have any idea as to the possible location or even the survival of all or part of Spalding's original manuscript. We had obtained copies of Spalding's known handwriting from Oberlin College, Ohio, where a collection of his materials rests, but we did not know where to look for the missing manuscript itself.

We knew from our background research that we had uncovered more testimony linking Spalding, Rigdon, Smith, and Smith's manuscript than had ever before been gathered in one place, and we knew that this constituted more than enough evidence to prove clearly that Spalding's second novel was the original source of *The Book of Mormon*. This evidence was conclusive enough to convince almost any person of the true origin of *The Book of Mormon*. However, no matter how many affidavits were produced, or how much circumstantial evidence was brought forward, the Mormon Church's response was that they would not believe the Spalding/Rigdon evidence unless Spalding's manuscript was produced in his own handwriting, paralleling *The Book of Mormon* exactly. And so we searched for this extra evidence.

Answer to a Critic's Argument

Critics of the Spalding/Rigdon thesis often asserted these same sentiments, even though they were not necessarily Mormons having a preconceived faith in *The Book of Mormon*. Fawn M. Brodie, who wrote the well-known biography of Joseph Smith, *No Man Knows My History*, dismissed the entire wealth of testimony which we and others have presented by saying of some of the affidavits presented to her:

> It may be noted that although five out of the eight had heard Spaulding's story only once, there was a surprising uniformity in the details they remembered after twenty-two years. Six recalled the names Nephi, Lamanite, etc., six held that the manuscript described the Indians as descendants of the lost tribes; four mentioned that the great wars caused the erection of the Indian mounds; and four noted the ancient scrip-

tural style. The very tightness with which Hurlbut here was implementing his theory rouses an immediate suspicion that he did a little judicious prompting.[1]

But Brodie has committed a common logical fallacy. To her there is no way in which *any* affidavits concerning the Spalding theory can be acceptable. If the testimonies agree with each other, this must have been "the result of collusion," but if the testimonies were not to agree with each other, there would be no case at all! Brodie needs to consider the realistic alternative—that the testimonies agree with each other because each person remembered the truth about what actually happened!

But eyewitnesses and testimonies, coupled with research into the movements of Spalding, Rigdon, and Smith, are not the only sources of evidence on which we base our conclusion. Even though the evidence already presented in this book is more than sufficient to convince us that Spalding's manuscript was taken by Rigdon, then revised and presented by Smith as the "Golden Bible," certain critics have not yet been satisfied. Brodie's book is an example of the opinion of some of these critics who reject the Spalding evidence.

The Two Manuscripts

When Hurlbut arrived at Clark's house in 1834 with a letter from Mrs. Spalding (now remarried as Mrs. Davison) giving him permission to remove the *Manuscript Found* from the trunk in which it had lain, he and Clark discovered it missing. All that was left in the old trunk were some assorted papers, including a short manuscript (one-sixth the length of *The Book of Mormon*) called *Manuscript Story*, which we have identified previously as Spalding's first attempt at writing a novel (but which was later abandoned for *Manuscript Found*, his second novel). This short, first novel was declared by Spalding's acquaintances and family to be different from Spalding's second novel, which they all identified as essentially *The Book of Mormon.*

John N. Miller, former boarder and employee of Spalding, stated in 1833, "I was soon introduced to the manuscripts of Spalding and persued them as often as I had leisure. He had written two or three books or pamphlets on different subjects; but that which more particularly drew my attention was one which he called the 'Manuscript Found.' "[2]

Miller was completely cognizant of the fact that *Manuscript Found* was not the only literary endeavor of Spalding. Aaron Wright corroborated this by saying, "Spalding had many other manuscripts."[3] Both of these men knew Spalding in Conneaut, Ohio, between 1809 and 1812—even before he moved to Pittsburgh or Amity, where he certainly did more writing. The often-voiced criticism that *Manuscript Story* was the only work of Spalding does not fit the evidence.

One affidavit which clearly shows that Spalding abandoned his first attempt and began his second novel, *Manuscript Found*, reads as follows: ". . . that he had altered his first plan of writing by going farther back with dates and writing in the old scripture style, in order that it might appear more ancient."[4]

To demonstrate that there were two manuscripts, and that it was the first of these that was found by Hurlbut in 1834 (*not* the one we identify with *The Book of Mormon*), the following excerpts from previously presented affidavits are given.

Rachel Miller, John Miller's daughter:
Father [John Miller] told him [D. R. Hurlbut] that the "Manuscript Found" was not near all of Spalding's writings. . . .

Mrs. McKinstry, Spalding's daughter:
The "Manuscript Found," she [Spalding's widow] said, was a romance. . . . She had no special admiration for it more than other romances he wrote and read to her.

As a further witness to the fact that it was Spalding's *second* novel which was identified by the witnesses as *The Book of Mormon,* and not his *first* novel, several witnesses made clear distinctions between these two novels. As an example, here is Spalding's daughter's statement, a short letter written on October 31, 1887, from Washington D.C.:

Dear Sir:
I have very carefully read the Rice Spalding manuscript *[Manuscript Story]* you gave me. It is not the "Manuscript Found," which I have often seen. It contained the words "Lehi," "Lamonia," "Nephi," and was a much larger work.
Respectfully,
Mrs. McKinstry[5]

Additional corroboration for the two-manuscripts thesis is provided from the collection of letters to President Fairchild of Oberlin College. These are letters written to Fairchild during the time immediately before and after he obtained possession of *Manuscript Story,* the first novel.

A.B. Deming, in a letter dated February 18, 1886, said:

There is a gentleman in this city [Chicago] who is over eighty years of age who formerly resided in Ohio. He had in his possession for ten days in Sept. 1871 The Lost Ten Tribes, a Manuscript which Solomon Spaulding wrote in New England before he came to Ohio. . . . I was in Washington D.C. 10 days Dec. and Jan. and gave Spaulding's daughter L.L. Rice's Story as Pub[lished] at Lamoni. She says it is not Manuscript Found.

A letter from L.L. Rice (to whom the manuscript belonged before it came to Oberlin College) to President Fairchild dated May 30, 1885, also gives a clue to distinguishing between *Manuscript Story* and *Manuscript Found*. In describing *Manuscript Story* he declared, "And there is no outcome of the quarrel, as the story is evidently unfinished, and stops abruptly." This could hardly have been the manuscript that was completely ready for publication and which lay in the Patterson Print Shop for such a long time—waiting for a preface, not a conclusion!

Fred Van Campen, a printer, wrote President Fairchild on June 3, 1885, and told of yet another manuscript by Spalding. Although the woman he speaks of was not Spalding's daughter-in-law, as he supposed (perhaps she was *John* Spalding's daughter-in-law), he could very well be right about the manuscript he describes:

Mrs. L.F. Spalding of this city, has in her possession a manuscript by the above author, entitled "A Romance of the Celes, or The Florentine Heroes, and the three Female Knights of the Chasm." with this there is a little book of scriptural quotations and comments.

Mrs. Spalding's husband was a son of Solomon Spalding. Solomon Spalding's widow was a resident of this city[a] before her death, which occurred in

---

[a]Again, this could not have been Solomon Spalding's widow, but may have been John Spalding's widow. The letter was written from Bay City, Michigan.

Rochester, N.Y. about eight years ago. The old lady was very fond of reading the manuscript to her neighbors, and several times tried to have it published, but could find no publisher who would take it on satisfactory terms.

Finally, the statement of R. Patterson to President Fairchild in his letter of March 9, 1885, sums up the rational attitude toward the two-manuscripts controversy:

Mrs. McKinstry, daughter of Rev. Solomon Spaulding still living at Washington D.C., in her testimony published in Scribner's Monthly by Mrs. E.E. Dickinson, states that her father wrote a number of romances as well as the one named "The Manuscript Found." The discovery of any of these other ms. would therefore not in any wise be inconsistent with the Rigdon-Spaulding theory of the origin of the so-called historical portions of the "Book of Mormon."

All of the above excerpts are in the possession of Oberlin College and may be read in the College library.

Our last testimony regarding *Manuscript Story* and *Manuscript Found* is another testimony given by Spalding's daughter. It is handwritten and is dated in Nomember of 1886. This could not be hailed as a forgery. It has never been published before and is more evidence to the truth of the Spalding/Rigdon thesis.

Mr. A.B. Deming,

Dear Sir,
I have read much of the Manuscript Story Conneaut Creek which you sent me. I know that it is *not* the Manuscript Found which contained the words "Nephi, Mormon, Maroni, and Laminites." Do the Mormons expect to deceive the public by leaving off the title page—Conneaut Creek and calling it Manuscript Found and Manuscript Story.

Mrs. M.S. McKinstry

Washington - Nov 3rd '86

Mr A B Deming

Dear Sir

I have read much of the manuscript Story Conneaut Creek which you sent me. I know that it is not the "manuscript Found" which contained the words "Nephi Mormon Maroni and Lamanites." Do the Mormons expect to deceive the public by leaving off the Title Page. Conneaut Creek and calling it manuscript Found and manuscript Story.

Yours M S McKinstry

The last statement of [illegible] previous adopted daughter with her signature,

A B Deming

The reason for establishing the important distinction between the two known novels of Spalding is that his *first* novel has been heralded by Mormons for years as "proof" that the minister's work was different from *The Book of Mormon.*

The Book of Mormon and Manuscript Found

Since Spalding's widow's copy of *Manuscript Found* was discovered missing sometime before 1834, and since the copy left with Patterson's business in Pittsburgh also disappeared, the Mormon Church evidently felt confident enough of the permanent loss of Spalding's *Manuscript Found* to stake their contention solely on the lack of a copy of this work. The church refused to accept the testimony of Spalding's contemporaries, declaring that until the manuscript (or a portion of it) was produced, circumstantial evidence was useless. Although that is far from the truth, as the consistency of the witnesses has shown, this has been the one fact barring the Mormon Church from accepting the truth of the Spalding/Rigdon evidence. The church pointed to the manuscript found by Hurlbut in 1834 as the only proof they felt was needed in order to prove that the Spalding/Rigdon thesis was wrong. However, aside from the direct statements by witnesses contending that Spalding's first novel was different from *Manuscript Found*, several witnesses stated directly (in fact, all those witnesses who mentioned the title at all) that the title of the second novel was *Manuscript Found*. For example, Solomon Spalding's brother, John, declared, "The book was entitled the Manuscript Found. . . ."[6] Henry Lake, Spalding's business partner in Conneaut, asserted, "He [Spalding] frequently read to me from a manuscript . . . which he entitled the 'Manuscript Found'. . . ."[7] Spalding's widow affirmed, "It [the manuscript] claimed to have been written by one of the lost nations . . . and assumed the title of 'Manuscript Found.' "[8]

Although it has been the position of the Latter Day Saints to claim that the *Manuscript Story* was the same as the *Manuscript Found*, and that there was no second novel, the circumstantial evidence alone makes such a position untenable. For example, a number of witnesses remember hearing unusual names from Spalding's second novel which are identical to names in *The Book of Mormon*. This striking duplication of unique names should convince even a skeptic of the common authorship of *Manuscript Found* and *The Book of Mormon*. Below are just five testimonies mentioning the same names in both works.

> It *[Manuscript Found]* gave a detailed account of their journey from Jerusalem under the command of Nephi and Lehi.[9]

> . . . the names of Nephi and Lehi are yet fresh in my

> memory, as being the principle heroes of his tale
> [*Manuscript Found*]. . . . Disputes arose in which
> caused them to separate into different bands, one of
> which was called Lamanites, and the other
> Nephites.[10]

> Some of the names that he mentioned while reading
> [*Manuscript Found*] . . . I have never forgotten. . . .
> They were: Mormon, Maroni, Lamenite, Nephi.[11]

> I have often heard him [J.N. Miller] tell about the
> Nephites and Zerahemlites before the "Book of Mor-
> mon" was published.[12]

> The names of Nephi, Lehi, Maroni, and in fact all the
> principal names, are brought fresh to my recollection
> by the Golden Bible [*Book of Mormon*]. . . . He
> [Spalding] landed his people near the Straits of Darien
> which I am very confident he called Zarahemla. . . .[13]

Perhaps we should be more inclined to believe the
Mormon contention that the similarities were coinciden-
tal if the names were more common ones, such as John or
James! It hardly seems possible that both Spalding and
Smith (or Moroni) could have independently arrived at
these names that are strikingly unusual, yet identical in
both *Manuscript Found* and *The Book of Mormon*. (See
Aaron Wright's cogent comments on this phenomenon.)[14]

In addition to this duplicate-name phenomenon, the
writing style of both books is identical. Scholars have
long criticized the bastardized King James English of
The Book of Mormon, lamenting the fact that Smith's
God was evidently addicted to Elizabethan speech
patterns! Portions of *The Book of Mormon* are copied
word-for-word from the King James Version of the Bible,
and there is a simple explanation of this phenomenon:
Solomon Spalding was addicted to King James English,

hoping that its use would help create that ancient atmosphere which might lend his novel the air of a "translation." Solomon's brother John said, "I well remember that he wrote in the old style."[15] R. McKee confirmed, "His style was flowing and grammatical, though gaunt and abrupt, very much like the story of the "maccabees" and other apocryphal books in the old Bibles."[16] As we have previously noted, Spalding's daughter stated that " 'The Manuscript Found, she [Spalding's widow] said, was a romance written in Biblical style. . . .'"[17]

Aaron Wright commented about the Conneaut period of Spalding's life that Spalding was addicted to the phrases "moreover" and "it came to pass," and we find that these phrases also occur repeatedly in *The Book of Mormon*. Abner Jackson recorded Wright's words for us: "When it *[The Book of Mormon]* was brought to Conneaut and read there in public, old esq. Wright heard it, and exclaimed, 'old come to pass has come to life again.' "[19] Joseph Miller's testimony informs us that Wright was not the only one to call Spalding "Old Come to Pass." Speaking of Spalding's residence in Amity, Pennsylvania, Miller said, "The words 'moreover,' 'and it came to pass,' occurred so often that the boys about the village called him 'old came to pass.' "[20] Henry Lake was perhaps the first (but by no means the last) to declare that *The Book of Mormon's* constant use of "and it came to pass" rendered it ridiculous. When speaking of Spalding's *Manuscript Found* he said, "I well recollect telling Mr. Spalding that the so frequent use of the words "and it came to pass," "Now it came to pass," rendered it ridiculous."[21]

Nor could coincidence explain the strikingly similar events described in both *Manuscript Found* and *The Book of Mormon*.

Joseph Miller:
Then on hearing read the account from the Book [Alma 2:3 of *The Book of Mormon*] of the battle between the Amalekites and the Nephites, in which the soldiers of one army had placed a red mark on their foreheads to distinguish them from their enemies [Alma 2:3 of *The Book of Mormon*] of the battle only the narrative, but the very words as they had been impressed on my mind by the reading of Spalding's Manuscript.[22]

Oliver Smith:
Nephi and Lehi were by him represented as leading characters when they first started for America. Their main object was to escape the judgments which they supposed were coming upon the old world.[23]

Henry Lake:
One time, when he [Spalding] was reading to me the tragic account of Laban [See I Nephi 3:28, 29] I pointed out to him what I considered an inconsistency, which he promised to correct, but by referring to the "Book of Mormon," I find to my surprise, that it stands there just as he read it to me then.[24]

John Spalding:
They afterwards had quarrels and contentions, and separated into two distant nations, one of which he denominated Nephites, and the other Lamanites. Cruel and bloody wars ensued, in which great multitudes were slain.[25]

Finally, both *Manuscript Found* and *The Book of Mormon* capitalized on the theme common to the period: the fate of the lost tribes of Israel. Many people during the nineteenth century contended that the lost tribes became either one of the European races or the Indians of the New World. One of the most popular exponents of this theory was James Adair, whose book *The History of the American Indians* was published in 1775. It is our belief that Spalding borrowed from Adair in

Manuscript Found, and that these same parallels still exist in *The Book of Mormon*. Some of these general paral lels were also noted between Spalding's *Manuscript Found* and *The Book of Mormon*.

> *Redick McKee:*
> I recollect quite well Mr. Spalding spending much time in writing . . . what purported to be a veritable history of the nations or tribes who inhabited Canaan. . . .[26]

> *Aaron Wright:*
> He [Spalding] showed and read to me a history he was writing, of the Lost Tribes of Israel. . . .[27]

> *Martha Spalding:*
> He had for many years contended that the Aborigines of America were the descendants of some of the lost Tribes of Israel and this idea he carried out in the book in question.[28]

> *John Spalding:*
> It was an historical romance of the first settlers of America, endeavoring to show that the American In- dians are the descendants of the Jews, or the Lost Tribes.[29]

The weight of such testimony is too much for the thin foundation of *The Book of Mormon.* Even if no portion of Spalding's second manuscript still existed today, the ob- jective student of history must acknowledge that Joseph Smith derived *The Book of Mormon* from Spalding's second novel.

We have the testimony of those who were familiar with Spalding's work, who identified his writing with *The Book of Mormon*. We have the testimony of those who knew that Spalding claimed Rigdon stole his manuscript, as well as the testimony of those to whom

Rigdon showed his clandestine manuscript. We have the testimony of those who placed Rigdon within reach of the Spalding novel at the time it was lost. We have the testimony of those who heard Rigdon allude to a "coming new religion." We have the testimony of those who knew that Rigdon and Smith were acquainted with each other long before Mormonism start ed, and long before Rigdon was "converted." We have the testimony of those who heard Rigdon preach Mormonism before his "conversion." The aggregate force of this testimony is overwhelming: *The Book of Mormon* was taken from Solomon Spalding's *Manuscript Found*.

In Appendix 8 we present parallels between Spalding's *first* novel, *Manuscript Story*, and *The Book of Mormon*. If there are numerous parallels between *these* two books, then it is certainly easy to see the connection between Spalding's literary concepts and *The Book of Mormon*. In the face of all this evidence, the Mormon Church contends that not a single such parallel exists, and that there is no connection at all between *The Book of Mormon* and the writings of Solomon Spalding. One of us, Wayne Cowdrey, is a former Mormon descended from Smith's scribe, Oliver Cowdery. Wayne Cowdrey was told by the Mormon Church that there is not one single parallel between the surviving Spalding work (his first novel) and *The Book of Mormon*. This claim sparked his curiosity. If true, Cowdrey could not use *Manuscript Story* as a key to unlock the mystery surrounding the origin of *The Book of Mormon*. But Cowdrey's study revealed to him that there were not just a *few* parallels between these two works, but *scores* of parallels! After discovering these parallels, Cowdrey made a firm resolution to leave the Mormon Church, and he presented some of these parallels at his "trial of excommunication."

The New Evidence

If we could actually find part of Spalding's *second* novel in his own handwriting, and if it were strikingly similar to *The Book of Mormon*, this would constitute additional proof that *The Book of Mormon* came from Solomon Spalding's *Manuscript Found*. This proof has now been supplied: *we have actually found twelve pages of the original Book of Mormon rendered in Solomon Spalding's own handwriting!* Howard Davis, who was the first of us to discover this startling new evidence, relates what happened to him in his research:

> In 1974 I began what was actually an aspiration of mine since 1964, to initiate a probe into the authorship of *The Book of Mormon*. In early January of 1975, Cowdrey and Scales joined me in this important endeavor. We frequently visited libraries and sent letters of inquiry to various areas of the United States. We later obtained from Mrs. Cowles, the Senior Cataloger at Oberlin College in Oberlin, Ohio, a photocopy of a deed in Spalding's handwriting, a business paper fragment in the same hand, and two unfinished letters of his. The college photographer then sent us twelve photographs of Spalding's *Manuscript Story*, in his handwriting, since the college possesses the original. The Mormon Church had previously refused our request for microfilm of the original *Manuscript Story*, saying they were not "authorized" to do so. We later obtained a complete copy of this first novel. I studied these specimens and handwriting analysis for many months. I knew that as a science, the art of examining questioned handwriting was exact and, in competent and experienced hands, conclusive evidence. Although I was certainly no expert and knew that my observations could not prove anything, I also knew that my study of the science would greatly facilitate our basic research. In early February of 1976, I was ill, home from work, but still

formed for the most ardent friendship & love.—Their acquaintance produced the most sincere attachment—They exchanged vows of perpetual fidelity & love to each other—& only waited for the termination of the war to fulfil their mutual engagement to unite their hands in wedlock—But their pleasing anticipation of conjugal felicity was destroyed by the cruel Sword of Sambal—Naught availed the innocence & the amiable accomplishments of the fair Heliza? She must fall a victim to satiate the revenge of a barbarous tyrant—Had Ilicion when he attacked the savage Monster, that had thus assassinated his beloved Heliza, it would have inspired him with the most ardent desire for revenge & added vigor to his arm & keeness to his sword.—A Kentuck Bard represented the evil form of Heliza as arriving on the celestial plain—& being told that she must wait a short time & Ilicion would ascend & conduct her as his partner to a delightful Bower which was surrounded by the most beautiful flowers & delicious fruits—& where the singing of musical Birds would charm them with their melody.—

When Elseon had entered the fort, he found that Lamosk with the survivors of his little band of warriors had made prisoners of the Sciotans whom Sambal had left to guard the imperial Ladies—& that these Sciotans had done them no injury nor even insulted them with words—Says Elseon for this honourable treatment of my friends I will shew these enimies compassion—Go says he to them, return in peace to your own land—& tell your friends that Elseon will not hurt an enimy, who has done him a favour.—

The time of Elseon was precious—He spent but a few moments with Lamesa, in which they exchanged mutual congratulations—& expressions of the most tender

MANUSCRIPT STORY

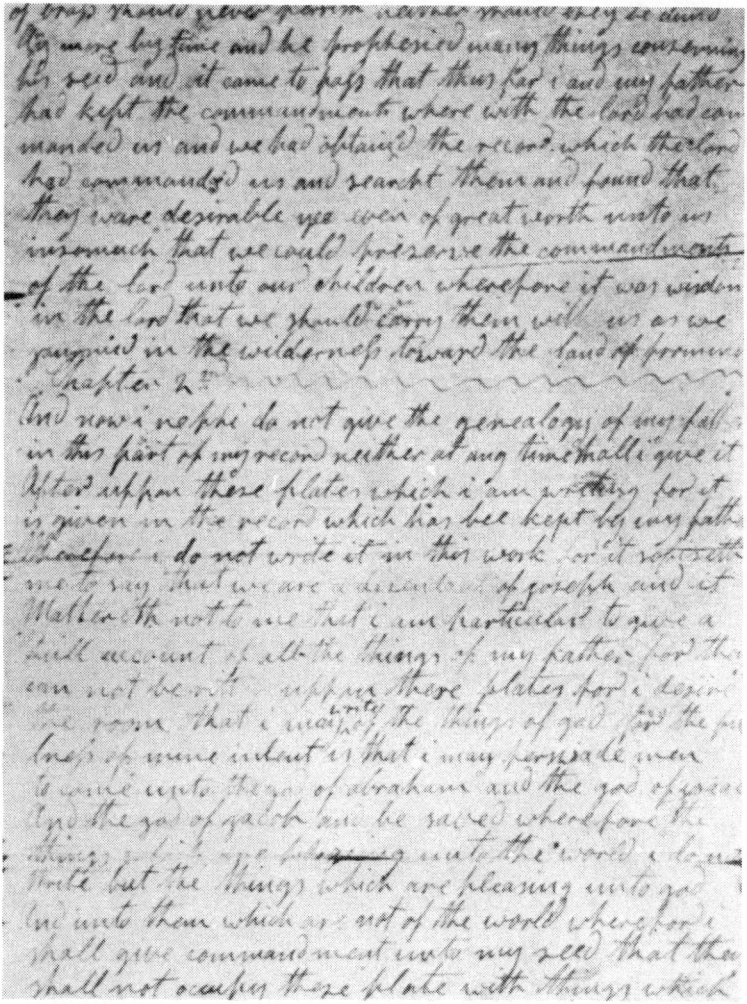

BOOK OF MORMON

studying. I absent-mindedly picked up a research book on Mormonism and flipped it open at random. On one page, in the lower left column, I spotted a photograph of an old manuscript. As soon as I looked at it, the thought flashed through my mind, "What is Spalding's handwriting doing here?" Then I read the caption: it turned out to be a picture of a section from the original transcribed copy of *The Book of Mormon*, now housed in the vault of the history office in Mormon headquarters in Salt Lake City, Utah.

I quickly contacted the Mormon Church and asked for copies of the portion of *The Book of Mormon* I was interested in, but was told that no copies would be made. I contacted some people I felt could help me, and they provided me with enough copies of the questioned material for us to examine. This was the breakthrough we were waiting for—almost three years of waiting.

The Trail of Preservation

What Davis had discovered was a portion of the original *Book of Mormon* known by the Mormon Church as the "unidentified scribe" section. The church had conducted a study to identify the several handwritings on the original manuscript, assigning the various portions to the appropriate scribes who took Smith's dictation when he supposedly translated *The Book of Mormon*. This one section, six sheets in length (twelve pages of writing) did not match the handwriting of any of the known associates of Smith. It was left labeled "unidentified scribe." Our studies have revealed Spalding to be that scribe.

But how did this section come to be in the original *Book of Mormon*? And why was this not discovered before?

After Smith dictated the manuscript of *The Book of*

Mormon (according to Mormon teaching), Oliver Cowdery, his principle scribe, wrote a second copy for the printer, which Cowdery kept until his death, at which time (March 3, 1850, Richmond, Missouri) it passed to his brother-in-law, David Whitmer, who kept it until his death on January 25, 1888. Fifteen years later, in April, 1903, G. Schweich sold the manuscript to the Reorganized Church for $2,450.

The original manuscript was kept closely guarded by Joseph Smith until 1841. On October 2, the cornerstone was being laid for a hospitality house in Nauvoo, Illinois. During the ceremony, Smith halted all activities and ran back to his own house. He reappeared moments later and brought the original *Book of Mormon* manuscript and placed it in a box, along with some other relics, in the cornerstone.

Writing of the event some years later, Elder F. Kesler, Sr., stated, "I saw the Prophet Joseph Smith Jr. hide up the above manuscript unto the Lord in the Southeast corner of the Nauvoo House, Illinois. I stood within eight or ten feet of him, heard and saw what he said and did, on that important occasion, which I freely testify to all the world."[31]

In 1882 Major Lewis C. Bidamon and his work crew were hired to dismantle the house and sell the brick. They found the old chest (10x14x18 inches) with its stone lid intact. They opened the chest with some difficulty and found the original manuscript, old but intact. On September 7, 1883, Mrs. Sarah M. Kimball was visiting Bidamon and procured twenty pages of the manuscript that were more legible than the rest of the manuscript. She stated that these twenty pages (ten sheets) were of a "finer texture, folded and sewed together."[32] These sheets are the best-preserved of the 144 pages which the Mormon Church possesses today. In 1970 Dean C. Jessee of the Mormon Church Historians' Office in Salt Lake City went to work trying to identify the various handwritings on the manuscript. He is the one who finally had to identify the writer of the Kimball acquisition as the "unidentified scribe." This group of twelve pages begins at I Nephi 4:20-37 and ends with I Nephi 11:32-12:8.[33] It is these twelve pages that we contend contain the handwriting of Solomon Spalding. There is no question of the authenticity of either *The Book of Mormon* manuscript or Spalding's known specimens of handwriting that we used in our comparison.

NAUVOO HOUSE

This is the Nauvoo House in Nauvoo, Illinois, where in October, 1841, Joseph Smith, Jr., deposited the original *Book of Mormon* manuscript containing the writings of the "Unidentified Scribe."

To confirm our own findings, we of course needed to obtain expert analysis of the questioned handwriting. Our months of handwriting study had enabled us to make the initial discovery of the similarities in the writing styles of the two works, and now we obtained expert testimony to confirm this handwriting discovery.

The sheets of *The Book of Mormon* section had been, according to the Mormons, de-acidified and laminated by the Barrows Restoration Shop in Richmond, Virginia, and therefore the exact dating of the pages based on paper-and-ink analysis was no longer possible. However, if the handwriting were shown to be the same, we would still be able to date *The Book of Mormon* pages before 1816, since Spalding died in that year, and the analysis would have shown him to be the author.

The First Reports

Henry Silver was the first Examiner of Questioned Documents that we hired, and the one with the greatest number of years of practice behind him. We had precise photocopies of the documents in our possession, and Silver's unreserved conclusion was based on these sheets. He studied the materials carefully and concluded:

Owing to the predominating number of definite similarities[b] pointed out under the preceding 8 points, between the said questioned handwriting in Exhibits A [the section of the Book of Mormon] and the said known handwriting or exemplars, in Exhibits B [the

---

[b]Similarity and dissimilarity are the two terms used by experts to indicate whether the comparisons show that the handwritings are identical.

known handwriting of Spalding from Ohio], it is my definite opinion that all the questioned handwriting in Exhibits A were written by the same writer, known as Solomon Spalding, who wrote his known handwriting in Exhibits B.

(We did not tell any of the experts initially what the examination pertained to, nor did we tell them what kind of verdict we wanted to hear.)

Howard Doulder was another expert we hired, and his first qualified report concurred in essence with Silver's report. (The Mormon Church later certified the photocopied documents as accurate representations of the originals.)

WILLIAM KAYE

William Kaye, a world-renowned Examiner of Questioned Documents, also studied the photocopied documents and concluded that both writings were executed by the same hand:

It is my considered opinion and conclusion that all of the writings were executed by Solomon Spalding, with the exception of the witnesses.[c]

On the strength of these three expert findings, we released this portion of our evidence to the public. Sufficient public pressure could then be brought to bear on the Mormon historians' office to permit the experts to view the original handwritten documents. After we made our findings public, the historians' office permitted the experts to view the originals.

The Second Reports

Silver was the first of the three experts to travel to Utah and see the original documents of *The Book of Mormon* section. We next arranged for him to travel to Ohio to view Spalding's known handwriting in the original documents kept at Oberlin College. Before this second trip, Silver experienced cardiovascular symptoms and was advised by his physician to discontinue the trip (see page 188 for physician's statement). However, Silver did render a second opinion, based on the photocopied documents. This report, also without reservation, completely supported his first statement and the first statements of the other two experts.

Doulder examined both sets of originals, but his second opinion contradicted his own first report as follows:

It is my conclusion the handwriting in the name of Solomon Spalding is NOT the author of the unidentified pages, listed as Q-1 thru Q-9 in this report of the Book of Mormon.

---

[c]The witnesses' signatures appeared at the end of a deed which Spalding had signed and which was one of the collection of Spalding's known writings kept at Oberlin College.

William Kaye made a trip to Ohio to view the known Spalding writing and to Utah to view the originals of the unidentified-scribe section of *The Book of Mormon*. Kaye's examination was the most extensive of the experts, since he not only made the trip to Ohio, but also made two trips to the Mormon originals in Utah. After countless additional hours spent in comparison of individual letters and words in the two sets of documents, comparing dissimilarities and similarities, Kaye rendered his second affirmative report, a summary of his exhaustive examination of the originals.[d] Kaye confirmed the common authorship of the two documents with the following statement:

> It is my considered opinion and conclusion and I believe that my examination to this point of the original documents concurs with my first report (which was based on photocopies originally provided me) and shows unquestionably that the questioned handwriting in the above named Mormon documents and the known handwriting in the above named Spalding documents undoubtedly have all been executed by the same person.

What is the verdict on the handwriting? The overwhelming weight of evidence shows that the unidentified section of *The Book of Mormon* is in the actual handwriting of Solomon Spalding.

What is the verdict on the Spalding authorship of *The Book of Mormon*? The evidence shows conclusively that Solomon Spalding is the actual source of the fictionalized history known today as *The Book of Mormon*.

---

[d]For example, Kaye examined the formation of over 2500 letter "T's" which occurred in the two sets of documents.

Henry Silver

QUALIFIED HANDWRITING EXPERT
EXAMINER OF QUESTIONED DOCUMENTS

June 4, 1976

Report to Howard Davis:

Re; Questioned handwriting on
parts of manuscripts.

Exhibits A - Four photocopies of parts of manuscript bearing the
questioned handwriting of the deceased known as
Solomon Spalding.

Exhibits B - Photocopies of 12 mages of manuscript known to have been
written around 1810 by the person known as Solomon
Spalding, so bearing his known handwriting.

Photocopies of two pages of a letter written to an unidentified friend, also bearing the known handwriting or
or exemplars of the deceased known as Solomon Spalding.

And photocopy of a Deed, dated Jan, 1811, bearing the known
handwriting, including the known signature of the person,
deceased, known as Solomon Spalding.

In comparing the said questioned handwriting in Exhibits A with the said
known handwriting or exemplars in Exhibits B. I find the following:

1. The peculiarity of form of the capital letters in the questioned
    handwriting, Exs. A, are definitely similar to that of the corres-
    ponding capitals in the said known handwriting or exemplars, Exs. B.

2. The peculiarity of forms of the small letters in the questioned
    handwriting, Exs. A, are definitely similar to that of the corres-
    ponding small letters in the exemplars, Exs. B.

3. The proportionate heights of the capital to small letters in the
    questioned handwriting, Exs. A, are definitely similar to that of
    the capital to small letters in the exemplars, Exs. B.

4. The forms of the links connecting the letters within words of the
    questioned handwriting, Exs. A, are definitely similar to the letter
    links connecting corresponding letters within corresponding words in
    the exemplars, Exs. B.

5. The width of spaces between letters of words in the questioned hand-
    writing, Exs. A, are definitely similar to the width of spaces
    between corresponding letters in corresponding words in the exemplars,
    Exs. A.

6. The base pattern or lineage of writing of the questioned handwriting,
    Exs. A, is definite similar to the base pattern or lineage of

Page 2.

writing of the exemplars, Exs. B.

7. The forms of ending strokes of words of the questioned handwriting, Exs. A, are definitely similar to that of the ending
strokes of corresponding words of the exemplars, Exs. B.

It is seen that the writer of the ending d's of words, of the
questioned handwriting, Exs. A, habitually made the ending strokes
of the said d's so that they ended ~~upward high~~ with high upward
strokes that turned leftward at their ends - the similar ending
of d's at the ends of words is seen in the exemplars, Exs. B.

8/ The angles of letter slants of the questioned handwriting, Exs. A,
are definitely similar to the angles of letter slants of corresponding letters in corresponding words of the exemplars, Exs. B.

CONCLUSION:

Owing to the predominating number of definite similiarities,
pointed out under the preceeding 8 points, between the said
questioned handwriting in Exhibits A and the said known handwriting or exemplars, in Exhibits B, it is my definite opinion
that all the questioned handwriting in Exhibits A were written
by the same writer, known as Solomon Spalding, who wrote his
known handwriting in Exhibits B.

Henry Silver
Handwriting Expert
Examiner of Questioned Documents

(Individual)

STATE OF CALIFORNIA
COUNTY OF Los Angeles } SS.
On June 7th 1976
before me, the undersigned, a Notary Public in and for said State, personally appeared
Henry Silver

to be the person ____ whose name____ is ____ subscribed _____ known to me
to the within instrument and acknowledged that ____ He
executed the same.
WITNESS my hand and official seal.
Signature
Mary Ann Brophy
Name (Typed or Printed)

FORM NO. 423-A 6/74

(This area for official notarial seal)

Howard C. Doulder

EXAMINER OF QUESTIONED DOCUMENTS
FINGERPRINT IDENTIFICATION

March 4, 1977

Dr. Howard A. Davis
Mr. Donald R. Scales
Mr. Wayne L. Cowdrey
of
Southern California

NATURE OF EXAMINATION

Handwriting examination and comparison.

DOCUMENTS EXAMINED

Q-1   ("A")   Machine copies and 16" X 20" photographic enlargements of
              handwriting.

              a.   "searched the Records", plus 36 lines of handwriting.

              b.   "rebelleth Against", plus 53 lines of handwriting.

              c.   "Repent and go", plus 32 lines of handwriting.

              d.   "partake of it also for i knew", plus 19 lines of
                   handwriting.

Q-2   (C)   One 16" X 20" photographic enlargement of only a portion
             of handwriting (center) "the full of all the Earth".

K-1   ("B")   Known Handwriting of "Solomon Spalding".

              12   Photographs 8" X 10" of which 6 are 16" X 20" enlargements,
                   bearing miscellenous handwriting.

              1   Machine copy, handwritten letter, 7 lines "Dear Parents",
                   also bears some figures on the upper right hand corner.

              1   Machine copy and 16" X 20" photographic enlargement,
                   bearing handwriting "Articles of Agreement" etc., and
                   the signature "Solomon Spalding", dated January 1811.

Report dated March 4th, 1977 - page 2

DOCUMENTS EXAMINED - Continued

      2 Pages of handwriting, machine copies and
         16" X 20" photographic enlargements, "But having every" etc.

NOTE:
    My mark of identification on the above documents I have examined are my
initials on the reverse side of each document in the lower right hand
corner.

RESULTS OF EXAMINATION

Because I have examined machine copies and photographic enlargements
and NOT the originals, I can only render an qualified opinion.

It appears because of individual writing characteristics, habits and
peculiarities the writer in the name of Solomon Spalding appearing as
listed on K-1 is one and the same writer and author of items listed as
Q-1 and Q-2.

A positive conclusion can be rendered only after an examination of all
the original documents.

                             Respectfully submitted,

                             Howard C. Doulder
                             Examiner of Questioned Documents

William Kaye
𝔈xaminer of 𝔔uestioned 𝔇ocuments
Special Document Photographs for Demonstration

August 27, 1976

Mr. Wayne Cowdrey
Howard A. Davis, P.H.D.
Mr. Donald R. Scales
25930 Rolling Hills Road
Torrance, Calif. 90505

Gentlemen:

Pursuant to your request, I have made an examination of certain xerox and photographic exemplars purported to be the uncompleted portion of the 1st Manuscript of Solomon Spalding, written about 1811-13. There are fifteen (15) documents on the 1st manuscript given to me for examination.

I have also received six (6) additional sheets of the purported written 2nd manuscript.

The purpose of this examination is an attempt to determine the following:

 Were all of the above written by one and the same person, Solomon Spalding?

 And if possible, to determine whether or not they were written at about the same time?

I have photographic enlargements made of all exemplar materials submitted to me for the use of making this examination.

It is my considered opinion and conclusion that all of the writings were executed by Solomon Spalding, with the exception of the witnesses.

In order to try and be more exacting as to the dating of the documents above described, it is of great importance that the purported original papers be presented to me for further examination, evaluation and research as to the kind of paper, parchment, etc. which was in existance on or about the years 1811-13.

Respectfully submitted

William Kaye
Examiner of Questioned Documents

Henry Silver

QUALIFIED HANDWRITING EXPERT
EXAMINER OF QUESTIONED DOCUMENTS

March 28, 1977

Report to Howard A. Davos: Re: Questioned handwriting.

Exhibits A - Five sheets bearing the questioned handwriting.

Exhibits B - Fifteen sheets bearing the known handwriting, as
             represented to me, of a known person, since deceased.

In comparing the said questioned handwriting, Exhibits A, with the
said known handwriting, Exhibits B, I find the following:

1. The base pattern or lineage of writing of corresponding words
   between the questioned writing, Exs. A, and the known writing,
   Exs. B, are definitely similar.

2. The angles of letter slants of corresponding words between Exs. A
   and Exs. B are definitely similar.

3. The peculiarity of forms of corresponding capital and small
   letters of Exs. A and Exs. B are definitely similar.

4. The proportionate heights of capital and small letters to each
   other in the questioned writing, Exs. A are definitely similar to
   that of the capital and small letters to each other in the
   known writing, Exs. B.

5. The forms of connecting links between letters of words in the
   questioned writing, Exs. A, are definitely similar to letter
   links between corresponding letters of words in the known writing,
   Exs. B.

6. The forms of ending strokes of words, some with the peculiarity
   of ending upward and curving to the left at the ends of words,
   are definitely similar in both Exhibits A and B.

CONCLUSION:
   Owing to the predominating number of definite similiarities,
   pointed out under the preceeding 6 points, between the said
   questioned handwriting in Exhibits A and the said known handwriting in Exhibits Exhibits B, it is my definite opinion that
   the questioned handwriting in Exhibits A were written by the
   same known person, as represented to me, who wrote his known
   handwriting in Exhibits B.

Henry Silver
Handwriting Expert
Examiner of Questioned Documents

Howard C. Doulder

EXAMINER OF QUESTIONED DOCUMENTS
AND FINGERPRINT IDENTIFICATION

September 15, 1977

Dr. Howard A. Davis
Mr. Donald R. Scales
Mr. Wayne L. Cowdrey
of
Southern California

NATURE OF EXAMINATION

Handwriting examination and comparison.

DOCUMENTS EXAMINED

During the month of February, 1977 at the request of Dr. Howard A. Davis,
Mr. Donald R. Scales and Mr. Wayne L. Cowdrey I made an examination of the
following documents.

Q-1 ("A") Machine copies and 16" X 20" photographic enlargements of handwriting.

      A.   "searched the Records", plus 36 lines of handwriting.

      B.   "rebelleth Against", plus 53 lines of handwriting.

      C.   "Repent and go", plus 32 lines of handwriting.

      D.   "partake of it also for i knew", plus 19 lines of handwriting.

K-1 ("B") E.   12 photographs 8" X 10" of which 6 were 16" X 20" enlargements,
            bearing miscellenous handwriting.

      F.   1 machine copy, handwritten letter, 7 lines "Dear Parents",
           also bears some figures on the upper right hand corner.

      G.   1 machine copy and 16" X 20" photographic enlargement, bearing
           handwriting "Articles of Agreement" etc., and the signature
           "Solomon Spalding", dated January 1811.

On March 4th, 1977 I sugmitted a written report with the following qualified opinion.

Qualifications:		*Memberships:*
Milwaukee Police Department	1947 – 1955	American Academy of Forensic Sciences
U.S. Treasury Department	1955 – 1973	Past Chairman Questioned Document Section
Private Practice since	1973	International Association for Identification, twice past chairman of the Questioned Document Section.

Page two:

RESULTS OF EXAMINATION

Because I have examined machine copies and photographic enlargements and
NOT the originals, I can only render a qualified opinion.

It appears because of individual writing characteristics, habits and
peculiarities the writer in the name of Solomon Spalding appearing as
listed on K-1 is one and the same writer and author of items listed as Q-1.

A positive conclusion can be rendered only after an examination of all the
original documents.

> Respectfully submitted,
> Howard C. Doulder

* *

On July 18th, 1977 I traveled to Oberlin, Ohio to examine the original writings
of Solomon Spaulding.

July 19th, 1977, 12:30pm to 4:30pm, Oberlin College Library, Seeley G. Mudd
Learning Center, Oberlin, Ohio I met with Mary E. Cowles, Senior Cataloger
(Special Collections) and was given for examination the original and machine
copy of Solomon Spaulding's Manuscript and the Library's copy of a deed signed
by Solomon Spaulding.

My examination was conducted visully and with magnification. I also took
photographs of various parts of the writings. Portions of pages 1, 2, 3, 4, 10,
11, 15, 20, 24, 37, 40, 53, 72, 93, 94, 111, 120, 148 and 160.

In the PM of July 19, 1977 I was enroute from Oberlin, Ohio to Salt Lake City, Utah.

July 20th, 1977, at the Mormon Church Office Building from 2:30pm to 4:30pm I
examined original documents bearing the following unknown handwriting.

from The Book of Mormon –

Q-1 1 Nephi, 4
    20. And after I had done this, I went forth unto the treasury of Laban.
       (etc. thru)
    37. And it came to pass that when Zoram had made an oath unto us,
       our fears did cease concerning him.

Q-2 1 Nephi, 4
    38. And it came to pass that we took the plates of brass and
       servant of Laban, and departed into the wilderness, and
       journeyed unto the tent of our father.

    1 Nephi, 5
     1. (thru)
    14. And it came to pass that my father, Lehi, also found upon the
       plates of brass a genealogy of his fathers; wherefore he knew
       that he was a descendant of Joseph; yea, even that Joseph who
       was the son of Jacob, who was sold into Egypt, and who was
       preserved by the hand of the Lord, that he might

Page three:

Q-3 1 Nephi, 5
           14. (cont.) Preserve his father, Jacob, and all his household from
               perishing with famine.

               (thru)

     1 Nephi, 7
           1. (thru)
           3. And it came to pass I, Nephi, did again with my

Q-4 1 Nephi, 7
           3. (cont.) brethren, go forth into the wilderness to go up to Jerusalem.

               (thru)

           17. But it came to pass

Q-5 1 Nephi, 7
           17. (cont.) that I prayed unto the Lord,

               (etc. thru)

           22. (and)
     1 Nephi, 8
           1. (thru)

           11. And it came to pass that I did go forth and partake of the fruit
               thereof; and I beheld that it was most sweet, above all that I
               ever before

Q-6 1 Nephi, 8
           11. (cont.) tasted. Yea, and I beheld that the fruit

               (etc. thru)

           27. And it was filled with people, both old and young, both male
               and female; and their manner of dress was exceeding fine; and they
               were in the attitude of mocking and

Q-7 1 Nephi, 8
           27. (cont.) pointing their fingers towards those who had come at
               and were partaking of the fruit.

               (thru)

     1 Nephi, 9
           1. (thru)

           4. Upon the other plates should be engraven an account of the
              reign of the kings,

Page four:

Q-8 1 Nephi, 9
      4. (cont.) and the wars and contentions of my people;

      (etc. thru)

  1 Nephi, 10
      1. (thru)
      11. And it came to pass after my father had spoken these words he spake
          unto myi brethren concerning the gospel which should be preached among
          the Jews, and also concerning the dwindling of the Jews in unbelief.
          And after they had slain the Messiah, who should come, and after he
          had been slain he should rise from the dead, and should make himself
          manifest, by the Holy Ghost,

Q-9 1 Nephi, 11
      1. For it came to pass after I had desired to know the things

      (etc. thru)

      18. And he said unto me: Behold, the virgin whom thous seest is the

NOTE: Also at this time I examined two or three other pages of handwriting,
       same in size, etc. However, I was not furnished with a copy of these
       nor could I photograph them.
       The handwriting appearing on these pages appeared to be the same writer
       as Q-1 thru Q-9.

At the time of my examination of the original writings I compared photographs
(mounted on poster board) and identified these to be true and accurate photographs
of Q-1 thru Q-9. (I placed my initials and date on the reverse side of each).

During the close of my examination I was permitted to take photographs of Q-5,
(1 Nephi, 7:17 thru 1 Nephi, 8:11), I took eight polaroid photographs with my
CU-5 camera.

RESULTS OF EXAMINATION

Examination of the original documents in comparison to machine copies and photographs
examined during February 1977 now showed in detail pen-lifts, line quality, letter
design, terminal spurs, connecting strokes, letter spacing and the alignment of
writing, plus other features needed to determine identification.

As I stated in my report dated March 4, 1977 of some writing similarities and letter
charateristics appeared both in the manuscript and the Book of Mormon. I now contribute
these similarities to the writing style of that century.

I have found writing and letter dis-similarities that are unexplainable and are not
attributed to individual writing variations of the same writer.

It is my conclusion the handwriting in the name of Solomon Spalding is NOT the
author of the unidentified pages, listed as Q-1 thru Q-9 in this report of the
Book of Mormon.

                        Respectfully submitted

                        Howard C. Ross-Doulder
                        Examiner of Questioned Documents

William Kaye

Examiner of Questioned Documents

Special Document Photographs for Demonstration

September 8, 1977

Wayne Cowdrey
Donald Scales
Howard Davis
c/o 1550 So. Anaheim Blvd. Suite C
Anaheim, Ca. 92805

Re: Questioned handwriting of
Book of Mormon manuscript

Gentlemen:

Pursuant to your assignment to me, I have been examining
the Mormon documents (Unidentified Scribe Section, Kimball Acquisition, Original Dictated Book of Mormon Manuscript) and the
Spalding documents (Conneaut Creek--Manuscript Story manuscript,
and assorted deeds and letters in his known hand) with a view to
determining whether or not the two sets of documents were written
by one and the same hand.

I have examined the original Spalding documents in Ohio
supplied by Oberlin College. In addition, I have examined the
original Mormon documents supplied by the Mormon Church in Salt
Lake City, Utah. I have also examined photostatic copies of both
sets of documents provided me by Oberlin College and the Mormon
Church. I have spent dozens of hours on the project and herewith
present a summary of my studies:

I have found numerous similarities between the Mormon documents that relate significantly to those I have found in the
Spalding documents. While a detailed report would require many
more hours of writing and comparison studies (for example, to
date I have carefully studied over 2500 letter "T's" in the two
sets of documents alone), my present opinion stands on my hours
of examination to this point. There are many similarities in
regard to certain letters and words that are present in the
Solomon Spalding manuscript and in the Book of Mormon manuscript.

It is my considered opinion and conclusion and I believe that
my examination to this point of the original documents concurs
with my first report (which was based on photocopies originally
provided me) and shows unquestionably that the questioned handwriting in the above named Mormon documents and the known handwriting in the above named Spalding documents undoubtedly have
all been executed by the same person.

Sincerely,

William Kaye

RODNEY B. KOVICK, M.D.
CENTURY CITY MEDICAL PLAZA
2080 CENTURY PARK EAST
LOS ANGELES, CALIFORNIA 90067
TELEPHONE (213) 277-0808
—
CARDIOLOGY AND INTERNAL MEDICINE

July 18. 1977

TO WHOM IT MAY CONCERN:

Mr. Henry Silver is a patient under my
care for angina pectoris secondary to
arteriosclerotic cardiovascular disease.
In view of his history, symptoms, and
physical findings, I have advised him
that it would not be in his best interest
to travel to Ohio at this time. I have
recommended against this, and advised
him to reduce his activity level until
his current medical condition is more
stable.

Very truly yours,

Rodney B. Kovick, M.D., F.A.C.C.

State license # G-20716

NOTES

1. Brodie, p. 447.
2. Howe, p. 283.
3. Ibid., p. 284.
4. Ibid., p. 288.
5. Deming, p. 25.
6. Howe, p. 279.
7. Ibid., p. 282.
8. Spalding, pp. 240-41.
9. Howe, p. 279.
10. Ibid., p. 280.
11. *Scribner's*, p. 615.
12. Deming, p. 4.
13. Howe, p. 283.
14. Ibid., p. 284.
15. Ibid., p. 280.
16. Washington, Pennsylvania, *Reporter*, Apr. 21, 1869.
17. *Scribner's*, p. 616.
18. Howe, p. 285.
19. Shook, p. 103.
20. Ibid., p. 103.
21. Howe, p. 282.
22. *Pennsylvania Telegraph*, Feb. 6, 1879.
23. Howe, p. 285.
24. Ibid., p. 282.
25. Ibid., p. 279.
26. Washington, Pennsylvania, *Reporter*, May 21, 1869.
27. Howe, p. 284.
28. Ibid., p. 280.
29. Ibid., p. 279.
30. *Manuscript Story*, Deseret Publishers, 1889.
31. Original Manuscript of the Book of Mormon, *Deseret Evening News*, Dec. 23, 1899.
32. Jessee, pp. 265-66.
33. Ibid., p. 273.
34. Ibid., p. 272.

Appendix 1

The Book of Abraham

On December 8, 1975, a well-respected and influential Mormon, Professor Dee Jay Nelson, resigned with his family from the Church of Jesus Christ of Latter Day Saints. His resignation was not based on any emotional, subjective feeling on his part, but was instead the result of his learned conclusions from his study of the original "Book of Abraham," a part of the Mormon sacred book *The Pearl of Great Price*.

The Book of Abraham was printed by the Mormon Church as a result of the supposed miraculous translation of some Egyptian papyri by Joseph Smith, Jr., of what he identified as writings by the Old Testament patriarch Abraham. For many years the original papyri with Smith's notes written on them were lost, and were presumed by the Mormon Church to have been destroyed in a fire in Chicago.

However, the papyri were eventually found in the Metropolitan Museum and given to the Mormon Church. The Mormons, through Hugh J. Nibley, asked Professor Nelson to translate the papyri, presumably hoping that his translation would support the divine authority of Joseph Smith as both prophet and translator. However, Professor Nelson discovered that an accurate translation of the materials showed them to be common burial papyri containing the Egyptian "Book of Breathings," a condensed form of the earlier "Book of the Dead." Not only did it have nothing to do with Abraham or Abraham's religion, but it was of a much later date than Abraham's time (about 1800 B.C.). This discovery, confirmed by several other Egyptologists, led Nelson to resign from the Mormon Church, since the church would not cooperate with Nelson's desires to have this discovery published to the world. His conclusions (in letter form) are appended here, as are the letters concerning his resignation.

PROF. DEE JAY NELSON
Lecturer
Egyptologist
719 HIGHLAND PARK DRIVE
BILLINGS, MONTANA 59102

Attention: First Presidency
Church of Jesus Christ of Latter Day Saints
Church Office Building
Salt Lake City, Utah

This letter is to inform you that it is our considered desire that my
own name and those of my wife and daughter be removed from the membership rolls of the Latter Day Saint Church.

We:

    Dee Jay Nelson
    Katherine G. Nelson (Mrs. Dee Jay Nelson)
    Kim Cherie Nelson
        do freely, and with full understanding of the implications
of the step, require that our names be removed from all member records
of the L.D.S. Church.

I, Dee Jay Nelson, do herby renounce and relinquish the priesthood
which I now hold.

Following my translation (the first to be published) of the bulk of
the hieratic and hieroglyphic Egyptian texts upon the Metropolitan-
Joseph Smith Papyri fragments three of the most eminent Egyptologists
now living published corroborating translations.   These amply prove
the fraudulent nature of the Book of Abraham, in which lies the un-
just assertion that negros are unworthy of participation in the highest
privileges of the L.D.S. Church.

We do not wish to be associated with a religious organization which
teaches lies and adheres to policies so blatantly opposed to the
civil and religious rights of some citizens of the United States.

By affixing our signatures to this document we exercise our constitutional rights of religious freedom and separate ourselves from the
Church of Jesus Christ of Latter Day Saints.

                           Dee Jay Nelson

                           Katherine G. Nelson

                           Kim Cherie Nelson

Date:

PROF. DEE JAY NELSON
Lecturer
Egyptologist
719 SHORLAND PARK DRIVE
BILLINGS, MONTANA 59102

February 15, 1976

Mr. R. L. Eardley
124 Lyman Ave.
Billings, Montana 59102

Dear Mr. Eardley,

Your certified letter of February 10, 1976 was received a few days
ago.   We found it offensive, implying by the word "court" that we
were to be judged.   The phrase which you used, "summoned to appear",
might better have been worded, "requested to appear" as we are no
longer under your jurisdiction.

My wife, my daughter and I have already resigned from the L. D. S.
Church by formal written notification addressed to the First Presidency
on December 8, 1975.

The scientific world finds the Book of Abraham an insult to intelligence.
Some of the most brilliant and qualified Egyptologists of our time
have labled it fraudulent upon the overwhelming evidence of the recently
discovered Metropolitan-Joseph Smith Papyri.   No truly qualified
Egyptologist has yet supported it.

We do not wish to be associated with a church which teaches lies and
racial bigotry.

Sincerely,

Dee Jay Nelson

JN/gh

PROF. DEE JAY NELSON
Lecturer
Egyptologist
719 HIGHLAND PARK DRIVE
BILLINGS, MONTANA 59102

AN OPEN LETTER

Dear Elder ⬛⬛⬛,

Your letter of November 12th was received. I read it with great interest. It is typical of many I get....pro and con.

I commend you upon your missionary work. Regardless of personal religious convictions this is laudable. The only way for man to truly serve God is to serve his fellow man. In this your efforts will stand you in good stead throughout life.

You presume too much in your letter....a characteristic of those who speak before learning all the facts. The first of several examples is shown in your question, "Why did you join the Church of Jesus Christ of Latter Day Saints in the first place?" Why should you assume that I joined the Church at all? I was born a Mormon, which is the poorest reason I know for being a member of any church.

Again you say that I am more impressed with wisdom than with religious truth. I fail to see the difference. I am a devoutly religious man. You need not doubt this. In fact, the best effort you have ever made to substantiate Christianity and the divine mission of Christ is insignificant compared to my own. In 1956-59 I walked every foot of ground that Jesus walked in order to learn more about Him. My life was often at considerable risk when it was necessary for me to travel as a Bedouin through Moslem territory forbidden to Christians. Years earlier I was a lay-scholar in what was then Palistine. I later expanded my knowledge as a student of Zakaria Ghoneim, Keeper of Antiquaties at Saqqara Egypt. I read nine ancient Middle and Far Eastern languages so you may assume that I have a good understanding of ancient history as well. This particularly includes Biblical history.

I further take umbrage with the implication that wisdom and Godliness cannot coexist. Surely your letter conveys this idea without intention. I can not believe you that foolish.

Is it inconceivable to you that I could be in possession of better information on Mormon background than you? I suggest that the best way to examine a fish bowl is from the outside. The view from within is distorted at best. The only honest way to evaluate any thesis is to step away from it and take the part of a critic. If it then meets all the measured tests you may comfortably embrace it with all your heart. I suggest, for instance, that you closely examine Joseph Smith's character at its source, as I have. Take a good look at his trial of 1826, in which he was convicted of fraud. You will find that the original trial clerk records still exist. Smith was, on this occasion, given full recourse to law and found guilty under fair examination.

In 1968 the L.D.S. Church First Presidency asked me to translate the newly discovered Joesph Smith Papyri Fragments. They did so with the knowledge that I was the most qualified member of the Church

to do so.   I promised that I would do it without editorializing
and in exchange received a promise that the Church would publish the
manuscript.   All I did - aside from commenting upon the age and
character of the papyrus (200B.C. to 100 A.D.) and explain meanings -
was convert the ancient Egyptian hieratic words to their English
equivalents.   It is not my fault that they did not say what Joesph
Smith claimed they did.   As I read the language with some ease there
is no possibility that I could be mistaken.   They are a remnant
of a much damaged form of ancient pagan funerary text.   One of them
was a copy of the'Per em Heru' (Book of the Dead) and the other a
copy of a'Sha/t en Sensen'(Book of Breathings).   That these were the
same papyri used by Smith can not be honestly denied because some of
the fragments were glued to pieces of heavy paper with hand written
notations on the back linking them to the "Prophet".   They also
display the original counterparts of hieratic characters which had been
copied by Smith (and or) his scribes into three hand written notebooks.
These notebooks are still in existance, owned by the Church.   I have
photo-copies of the pages.

Of particular importance is the original of Facsimile No. 1.
(printed in all editions of the Book of Abraham) among the papyri
fragments.   This fact has been freely admitted by the Church.
I wonder at the exclusion, from the Book of Abraham, of the four vertical
lines of hieroglyphic writing which boarder both sides of the original
vignette.   I should think that Joseph Smith, 'being a self-avowed
expert on the Egyptian language', would have thought them vital (in
an otherwise hieratic manuscript).   These four lines are literally
caption data dealing with the individuals shown in the picture.
Smith's explanation insists that this is a picture of Abraham on
an altar of sacrifice.   The original caption states otherwise, telling
that the man on the "Funerary bier" is a pagan priest of Osiris named
"Hor".   The same name can be clearly read in two places on printed
copies of the Book of Abraham, Facsimile No. 3.

Despite their promise,the Church fathers refused to publish my
translation so, upon threat of excommunication, I procured private
publication by Modern Microfilm Co., Salt Lake City.   My excommunication was repeatedly ordered and withdrawn over the next several
years.   I remained in the Church only because I thought that a
voice of an elder in the brotherhood would have more impact than
otherwise.   Also I do not like to be threatened.   In December
1975 the order again came so I sent my resignation.   I was commanded
to appear before a local Bishop's court of examination.   In a
telephone conversation with the Stake President I agreed to come
with one proviso. All I required is that a committee of one or more
persons be sent to examine the massive documentation which I have
collected to prove that the Book of Abraham in the Pearl of Great
Price is untrue.   I asked only one hour of the valuable time of
such a committee.   A letter to the Stake President with the same
proposal was never answered.   I promised a respectful reception to
the committee.   No representative was ever sent so I did not appear.

The proceedures of these excommunication "trials" are illegal
under written regulations of the Church itself, which insists that
it is governed by rules which do not conflict with the constitutional
rights of citizens.   Despite this, the "trials" do not offer the
right of defense and rebuttal to the persons being examined.   This
is a clear infringement upon the constitutional privilege.   Several

friends, who dared to question L. D. S. teachings, have been subjected to gross miscarriages of justice in their excommunicational "trials". Among these were devoutly Christian men like Dr. John Fitzgerald and Grant Heward.

I have now published five books and booklets on the Book of Abraham question. The last of these was in collaboration with John Fitzgerald.

Truth is the positive side of reality, which has a second pole. You can not assess the value of any belief without first considering the other viewpoint in an open minded way. No one man is the possessor of all truth. On the other hand ignorance is not the absence of knowledge. It is rather, the massive misuse of information.

Let me ask, where is the Egyptologist who will support the Book of Abraham? My translation was later supported by the published translations of 3 of the greatest living Egyptian philologists. Since the turn of this century a dozen of the best Egyptologists have refuted the Book of Abraham, including Sir W. Flinders Petrie, the father of modern Egyptology.

Some letters ask how I could dare disagree with Dr. Hugh Nibley, whom they call the ultimate authority. While I greatly admire Nibley I can hardly acknowledge him as any kind of an authority on matters Egyptian. I have honestly refered to him as a talented amateur. In several of his own publications and lectures he has refered to himself as "not qualified as an Egyptologist". He is an honest man which is well demonstrated by the way he invariably talks in circles about the Book of Abraham without getting to a definable point.

If the veracity of the Book of Abraham were to be tested in any court in the land the mountain of evidence would easily overthrow it. You have said that when you read it your heart burns within you and that this is your proof of its authenticity. The hard facts simply do not support that collection of bigoted nonsense called the Book of Abraham. If it makes your heart burn to read it then I recommend the Arabian Nights. One is no more outlandish than the other. Do you doubt that the ancient Egyptian heart burned any less warmly when he read the Book of the Dead, and how often have I heard Moslems say the same.

I invite you or anyone else to show me the error of my findings. Of course, to do so you must closely examine my documentation at the risk of your own convictions. I have been on both sides of the issue. Don't question anything until you can say the same.

The Mormon Church is a great humanitarian organization and this is a good thing. It does, however, teach false history and a thesis which says that negros are (in some ways) debased humans by virtue of their race. How does your bosom burn when you swallow that Christian pill?

Look at all the facts before you are so sure of yourself.

May the grace of God be upon you in all things good and may you prosper in His word. This I pray, with the hope that He will forgive me for dipping my pen too deeply in acid.

Appendix

Joseph Smith, Peepstone Gazer

In 1826, Joseph Smith was still engaged in fortune-telling by means of stones into which he would gaze and claim to see hidden treasure and other things desired by his clients. Published court records from that time show that Smith was convicted on March 20, 1826, in Bainbridge, Chenango County, New York. Peter G. Bridgman brought suit against Smith, claiming that he had used fraudulent means ("glass-looking") to make money from Bridgman. The entire court record (except for the sentencing record) is reproduced in Brodie's book *No Man Knows My History* (pp. 427-49). This is proof that Smith was already engaged in finding secrets by means of stones as early as 1826, long before he was supposedly given the "Urim and Thummim" stones by Moroni to aid in "translating" *The Book of Mormon*.

For many years Mormons have tried to claim that the printed court record could not be relied on, since the original was missing. The proof needed to convince the skeptical Mormons was to be found in the original writing of the court. Wesley P. Walters, investigator of early Mormon sources, found two documents that completely vindicated the court record previously printed. Walters found both the judge's records and the record of Constable DeZeng, who served the warrant on Smith. De Zeng's warrant record for Chenango County is dated 1826, and one line reads, "Serving Warrant on Joseph Smith. . . ." Judge Albert Neely's bill dated Smith's trial at March 20, 1826, the same date reported on the published court record. The entire record on the sheet in question is reproduced here to settle the record once and for all.

In addition, Walters has also recently found (in the Turner Collection of the Illinois State Historical Library in Springfield, Illinois) a letter from a judge who was familiar with this case and its outcome. The letter was written in 1842 by Judge Joel King Noble, a justice of the peace in Colesville, Broome County, New York. Noble's letter clearly states that Smith was not only found guilty, but, in his words, was "condemned." Noble explained that Smith was not sentenced, since it was his first offense and he was so young that his mandatory departure from the city was considered sufficient sentence.

These records corroborate the testimony given by many of Smith's neighbors in Palmyra to the effect that Joseph Smith's occupation up until the time of Mormonism was the dubious trade of "treasure-seeker and glass-looker."

Chenango County to Albert Neely Dr.

People
vs Barney   } Assault & Battery
               Trial at G.A. Sen...
               Witness
               James Humphrey
               Lee and Task...
               Albert Neely
               To my fees in trial
               of above Cause   } 3, 68

People
vs
Samuel May   } Assault & Battery
March 22. 1826   To my fees in this Cause — $1,99

Same
vs
Joseph Smith   } Misdemeanor
The Glass Looker
March 20. 1826   To my fees in examination
                  of the above Cause   } 2, 68

Same
vs
Moses Evans   } Champerty
Feb 2. 1826   To examination of above Cause 2, 18

— Evans   } Assault & Battery
                  To my fees in above Cause — 1, 46

Same
vs
Robert Farnell } Petit Larceny
Oct 3. 1826   To my fees in above Cause — 1, 85

Same
vs
Isa Churchill   } Assault and Battery
Nov 9. 1826   To my fees in above Cause — 2, 53
                  Albert Neely, Jus. of Peace $18, 37

Appendix

Matilda Spalding's Testimony

Of all the affidavits presented in this study, that of Mrs. Matilda Spalding Davison (Spalding's widow) as printed in *The Boston Recorder* in 1839 had aroused the most controversy. It is pointed out by Mormons that Mrs. Spalding, of all the people who knew Spalding, would presumably know more details of the fate of *Manuscript Found* than anyone else. The Mormons point to certain apparent problems with her testimony and dismiss the whole thesis as spurious.

However, there are no insurmountable problems with her testimony; we need only examine the "problems" in context and in the light of the other testimony in order to find that a few minor inconsistencies do not affect the basic premise at all. With this in mind, we here reprint the entire statement, noting the areas of concern and then presenting what we consider to be valid reconciliations of the problems.

ORIGIN OF THE "BOOK OF MORMON," OR "GOLDEN BIBLE."

As this book has excited much attention, and has been put by a certain new sect in place of the sacred Scriptures, I deem it a duty which I owe to the public to state what I know touching its origin.

That its claims to a divine origin are wholly unfounded, needs no proof to a mind unperverted by the grossest delusions. That any sane person should rank it any higher than any other merely human composition is a matter of the greatest astonishment: yet it is received as divine by some who dwell in enlightened New England, and even by those who have sustained the character of devoted Christians. Learning recently that Mormonism has found its way into a church in Massachusetts, and has impregnated some of its members with some of its gross delusions, so that excommunication has become necessary, I am determined to delay no longer doing what I can to strip the mask from this monster of sin, and to lay open this pit of abomination. Rev. Solomon Spalding, to whom I was united in marriage in early life was a graduate of Dartmouth college, and was distinguished for a lively imagination and a great fondness for history. At the time of our marriage he resided in Cherry Valley, New York. From this place we removed to New Salem, Ashtabula county, Ohio, sometimes called Conneaut, as it is situated upon Conneaut creek. Shortly after our removal to this place, his health sunk, and he was laid aside from active labors. In the town of New Salem there are numerous mounds and forts, supposed by many to be the dilapidated dwellings and fortifications of a race now extinct. These ancient relics arrest the attention of the new settlers, and become objects of research for the curious. Numerous implements were found, and other articles, envincing great skill in the arts. Mr. Spalding being an educated man and passionately fond of history, took a lively interest in these developments of antiquity, and in order to beguile the hours of retirement and furnish employment for his lively imagination, he conceived the idea of giving an historical sketch of this long lost race. Their extreme antiquity of course would lead him to write in the most ancient style; and as the Old Testament is the most ancient book in the world, he imitated its style as nearly as possible. His sole object in writing this historical romance was to amuse himself and his neighbors. This was about the year 1812. Hull's surrender at Detroit occurred near the same time, and I recollect the date well from that circumstance. As he progressed in his narrative, the neighbors would come in from time to time to hear portions of it read, and a great interest in the work was excited among them.

It is claimed to have been written by one of the lost nation, and to have been recovered from the earth, and assumed the title of "Manuscript Found." The neighbors would often inquire how Mr. Spalding progressed in "deciphering" the "Manuscript," and when he had a sufficient portion prepared, he would inform them and they would assemble to hear it read. He was enabled from his acquaintance with the classics and ancient history to introduce many singular names, which were particularly noticed by the people, and could be easily recognized by them. Mr. Solomon Spalding had a brother, Mr. John Spalding, residing in the place at the time, who was perfectly familiar with this work, and repeatedly heard the whole of it read.

From New Salem we removed to Pittsburgh, Pa. Here we found a friend in the person of Mr. Patterson, an editor of a newspaper. He exhibited his manuscript to Mr. P., who was very much pleased with it, and borrowed it for perusal. He retained it for a long time and informed Mr. S. that if he would make out a title page and preface, he would publish it, and it would be a source of profit.

This Mr. S. refused to do, for reasons which I cannot now state. Sidney Rigdon, one of the leaders and founders of the sect, who had figured so largely in the history of the Mormons, was at this time connected with the printing office of Mr. Patterson, as he is well known in that region, and as Rigdon himself has frequently stated. Here he had ample opportunity to become acquainted with Mr. Spalding's manuscript, and to copy it if he chose. It was a matter of notoriety and interest to all who were connected with the printing establishment.At length the manuscript was returned to its author, and soon after we removed to Amity, Washington County, Pa., where Mr. S. deceased in 1816. The manuscript then fell into my hands, and was carefully preserved. It has frequently been examined by my daughter, Mrs. McKinstry, of Monson, Mass., with whom I now reside, and by other friends. After the "Book of Mormon" came out, a copy of it was taken to New Salem, the place of Mr. Spalding's former residence, and the very place where the "Manuscript Found" was written. A Mormon preacher appointed a meeting there, and in the meeting read and repeated copious extracts from the "Book of Mormon." The historical part was immediately recognized by the older inhabitants before. Mr. John Spalding was present, who is an eminently pious man, and recognized perfectly the work of his brother. He was amazed and afflicted that it should have perverted to so wicked a purpose. His grief found vent in a flood of tears, and he arose on the spot and expressed in the meeting his deep sorrow and regret that the writings of his sainted brother should be used for a purpose so vile and shocking. The excitement in New Salem became so great that the inhabitants had a meeting and deputed Dr. Philaster Hurlbut, one of their number, to repair to this place and to obtain from me the original manuscript of Mr. Spalding, for the purpose of comparing it with the Mormon Bible to satisfy their own minds and to prevent their friends from embracing an error so delusive.

This was in the year 1834. Dr. Hurlbut brought with

him an introduction and request for the manuscript, signed by Messrs. Henry Lake, Aaron Wright, and others, with all of whom I was acquainted, as they were my neighbors when I resided in New Salem.

I am sure that nothing could grieve my husband more, were he living, than the use which has been made of his work. The air of antiquity which has been thrown about the composition, doubtless suggested the idea of converting it to purpose of delusion. Thus an historical romance, with the addition of a few pious expressions and extracts from the sacred Scriptures, has been constructed into a new Bible, and palmed off upon a company of poor deluded fanatics as divine.

I have given the previous narration, that this work of deep deception and wickedness may be searched to the foundation and its author exposed to the contempt and execration he so justly deserves.

(Signed)
Matilda Davison

Rev. Solomon Spalding was the first husband of the narrator of the above history. Since his decease she has been married to a second husband, by the name of Davidson. She is now residing in this place, is a woman of irreproachable character, and a humble Christian, and her testimony is worth of implicit confidence.

A. Ely, D.D.
Pastor of the Congregational Church, Monson.
D. R. Austin, principal of Monson Academy.
Monson, March 1, 1839.

1. Mrs. Davison said that the novel her husband was working on was written in "the most ancient style," although other testimony states that his *first* novel (*Manuscript Story*) was not written in biblical style, but

that his *second* novel was. However, Mrs. Davison's credibility at this point is not damaged at all, since she appears at this point to be simply ignoring the first novel. Mrs. Davison was not unaware of Spalding's first novel, for her daughter stated that she "had no special admiration for it [Manuscript Found] more than other romances he wrote and read to her."

2. As is common in husband-wife relationships, the two parties often have divergent views on their financial status. Although Mrs. Davison says that Spalding's sole object was nonfinancial, while others said that his object was a futile attempt to make enough money to repay some of his debts, we need not consider this a serious obstacle to the widow's credibility. Often husbands (especially at that time) were reluctant to worry their wives with the true financial condition of the family. Perhaps Spalding never told Matilda their true financial condition. Or perhaps he did, but she, being properly reticent about her family's personal affairs, felt that their poverty was their own business.

3. Again referring to number 1, Mrs. Davison's identification of the novel as *Manuscript Found* and her ignoring of *Manuscript Story* cannot be construed as an assertion that only one novel ever existed, to her knowledge. Her daughter's remembrances, along with those of others, show clearly that this present testimony is concerned only with the novel identified with *The Book of Mormon*; for this reason Mrs. Davison felt no need to mention any other compositions by her husband.

4. Although the only testimony we have from Patterson does not indicate that he was "a friend" of Spalding, we must remember that there were *two* Patterson brothers in the publishing firm, and it certainly could have been the other Patterson brother with whom Spalding was more closely acquainted.

5. Other testimony shows that Patterson required a fee to publish Spalding's novel, and if our conjecture that he had not told his wife of their overall financial distress is true, then it would be logical for him to keep this information from her also. This does not indicate that what she said was incorrect, but only that she did not possess every detail of information.

6. According to her daughter, Mrs. Davison was not overly interested in her husband's novels, and therefore it is understandable that she was unaware that Spalding's manuscript had not been returned from the printshop, but was lost and presumed by her husband to be stolen by Rigdon. Evidently Spalding had two copies of the novel, one of which was lost at the printshop and the other of which he kept and which his wife found after his death and supposed it to be the same one as had been at the printshop.

7. As Rigdon pointed out, Hurlbut was not a doctor, but had been called that by his mother. One could hardly fault Mrs. Davison for thinking he was a doctor, since she met him on only one occasion and never heard from him after that time. Their discussion would hardly have been on the topic of Hurlbut's name, since he came only to obtain a copy of Spalding's novel from his widow.

8. Since Hurlbut never contacted Mrs. Davison again, there was no way for her to know that he did not receive the second novel, but that only the first novel was left in the trunk when he opened it.

Our examination of the so-called "problems" in Mrs. Davison's testimony show that they can all be answered easily, without damaging either her testimony or good rules of evidence, and that the basic facts of her affidavit will stand careful examination.

Finally, the contention that the entire affidavit was spurious, and not even produced by Mrs. Davison, has been raised. This challenge arose because it was stated that she did not write a statement herself, and this was misconstrued to mean that the statement itself was not authentic. But what actually happened is that Mrs. Davison *dictated* her thoughts to Messrs. Austin and Storrs and then *signed* the subsequent record. The following statements clarify this occurrence.

Sturbridge, Mass., June 28th, 1841.

The circumstances which called forth the letter published in the Boston Recorder in April 1839, were stated by Mr. Storrs in the introduction to that article. At his request I obtained from Mrs. Davison a statement of the facts contained in that letter, and wrote them out precisely as she related them to me. She then signed the paper with her own hand which I have now in my possession. Every fact as stated in that letter was related to me by her in the order they are set down. (There is one word mis-printed in the published letter—instead of "woman preacher," on the second column, it should be Mormon preacher.)

That the pamphlet published to refute the letter should contain false statements is not surprising. A scheme got up in falsehood must be sustained by lies. But the truth of the statements contained in that letter of Mrs. D. will remain unshaken, notwithstanding all the Mormons can do. It gives a very clear, consistent and rational account of the origin of that abominable piece of deception and fraud.

Mrs. Davison is now living about twelve miles from this place; is an aged woman and very infirm.[a]

Dr. R. Austin

Dr. Clark wrote Rev. Storrs and received the following reply, which is an extract of that letter:

---

[a]Clark, *Gleanings by the Way*, pp. 264-66.

It is very true Mrs. Davison did not write a letter to me, and what is more, of course she did not sign it. But this she did do, and just what I wrote you in my former letter I supposed she did: she did sign her name to the original copy as prepared from her statement by Mr. Austin. This original copy is now in the hands of Mr. Austin. This he told me last week.[b]

> Your brother in the Lord,
> John Storrs.

So what transpired was that Storrs wrote Austin at Monson, and he in turn took down Mrs. Davison's words, and then she examined the letter and signed it. The signed letter was in Mr. Austin's possession for a number of years, so that anyone could have examined it and even spoken to Mrs. McKinstry or Mrs. Davison about this matter.

---

[b]Ibid., p. 259.

Appendix

The Eight
Witnesses at Conneaut

In the past, Mormon critics of the Rigdon/Spalding thesis have alleged that those witnesses who provided affidavits in support of the thesis were untrustworthy. Some Mormons have even said that the witnesses in Conneaut were scoundrels who would lie just to get attention.

We have carefully investigated the backgrounds of the various witnesses and have found, based on the evidence, that these witnesses, *especially* the Conneaut ones, were completely above reproach in all of their conduct and could be trusted to testify to what they actually knew. As an example of the outstanding moral character of the witnesses we have presented, we have reproduced here character references for the eight witnesses from Conneaut. These testimonials are examples of the high regard in which these people were held by their peers in the community.

THE STATE OF OHIO
LAKE COUNTY

Before me, a notary public in and for said county, personally appeared J. H. Britton, who, being duly sworn, on his oath says:

That he is now a resident of Painesville in said county, and is now of the age of seventy-two years: was born in the town of Van Buren, Onondaga Co., N.Y., and he further says: I was living in my father's home in the township of Richmond, Ashtabula Co., O., from about 1836 until about 1848, and during that time I became and was acquainted with Aaron Wright and Henry Lake, two of the persons who have furnished statements as to the origin of the Book of Mormon; which statements are published in E. D. Howe's "History of Mormonism" or "Mormonism Unveiled," published at Painesville, O., in 1834; that I knew said Wright and Lake well, that they were men of good reputation for truth and veracity, and were in every way well esteemed and respected in the community where they lived. Mr. Wright then lived in the village of Conneaut, in said county, and was one of the pioneers of the vicinity, and a large owner of real-estate, and owned a flouring-mill which was reported to be the first mill of its kind built in that vicinity. Mr. Lake also lived near Mr. Wright, and was also one of the first settlers of the vicinity. And further affiant sayeth not.

J. H. Britton

Subscribed in my presence and sworn to before me this 22d day of June, 1905.

G. N. Tuttle
Notary public in and for said county[a]

------

[a]Shook, p. 113.

E. D. Howe made a statement concerning the witnesses after he had interviewed everyone he could who was living in Conneaut at the time Spalding was there. He made his investigation in 1834 and stated the following on page 281 of his book:

> We might therefore introduce a great number of witnesses, all testifying to the same general facts; but we have not taken the trouble to procure the statements of but few, all of whom are the most respectable men, and highly esteemed for their moral worth, and their characters for truth and veracity are unimpeachable. In fact, the word of any one of them would have more weight in any respectable community, than the whole family of Smiths and Whitmers, who have told about hearing the voice of an angel.[b]

Rev. John Hall was the rector of St. Peter's Church at Ashtabula, Ohio, and was closely acquainted with most of the witnesses from Conneaut and with their truthfulness. His statement, while brief, supports their reliability.

> As to the deponents in reference to the Spalding manuscript, at New Salem (now Conneaut). I have been acquainted with them for 30 years (excepting Miller), and they are respectable persons.
> > (Signed)
> > John Hall, Rector of S. Peter's
> > Ashtabula, Ohio.[c]

Although Hall was not able to render a verdict on Miller's character, Rev. J. W. Hamilton was well-acquainted with him and had this to say concerning his morals:

---

[b]Howe, p. 281.
[c]Clark, p. 9.

Some time since I became the owner of the book of Mormon. I put it into the hands of Mr. Joseph Miller, Sr., of Amwell township. After examining it he makes the following statement concerning the connection of Rev. Solomon Spaulding with the authorship of the book of Mormon. . . . Mr. Miller is now in the seventy-ninth year of his age. He is an elder in the Cumberland Presbyterian Church. His judgment is good and his veracity unimpeachable. He was well acquainted with Mr. S. while he lived at Amity. He waited on him during his last illness. He made his coffin, and assisted to bury his remains where they now lie, in the Presbyterian graveyard at Amity. He also bailed Mr. S.'s wife when she took out letters of administration on his estate.

Mr. Miller's statement may be relied on as true.

J. W. Hamilton[d]

Another tribute to Miller's character was given by Dr. Sharp to the *Washington Reporter*:

But we have a living witness—Joseph Miller—a veteran of the war of 1812. A Christian gentleman of undoubted veracity, with mind and memory remarkable for their prolonged preservation, and singularly free from any signs of senility. I had an interview with Mr. Miller two days . . . .[e]

Dr. Sharp reported in the same article that Miller had told him before the official interview started ". . . that he would not intentionally say one word that he did not believe to be strictly true. . . ."

Shortly after *The Book of Mormon* was published, Spalding's landlord from Conneaut, Oliver Smith, was persuaded to give his testimony concerning Spalding's novel and its similarity to *The Book of Mormon*.

---

[d]Creigh, pp. 89-93.
[e]*Pittsburgh Telegraph*, Feb. 6, 1879, p. 1, "The Book of Mormon."

Conneaut, August 1833

When Solomon Spaulding first came to the place, he purchased a tract of land, surveyed it out, and commenced selling it. While engaged in this business, he boarded at my house, in all nearly six months. All his leisure hours were occupied in writing an historical novel, founded upon the first settlers of this country. He said he intended to trace their journey from Jerusalem, by land and sea, till their arrival in America; give an account of their arts, sciences, civilization, wars, and contentions. In this way, he would give a satisfactory account of all of the old mounds so common to this country. During the time he was at my house, I read and heard read one hundred pages or more. Nephi and Lehi were by him represented as leading characters, when they first started for America. Their main object was to escape the judgments which they supposed were coming upon the old world. But no religious matter was introduced as I now recollect. Just before he left this place Spaulding sent for me to call on him, which I did. He then said that although he was in my debt, he intended to leave the country, and hoped I would not prevent him. For, says he, you know I have been writing the history of the first settlement of America, and I intend to go to Pittsburgh, and there live a retired life, till I have completed the work, and when it is printed, it will bring me a fine sum of money, which will enable me to return and pay off all my debts. The book, you know, will sell, as every one is anxious to learn something upon that subject. This was the last I heard of Spaulding or his book, until the Book of Mormon came into the neighborhood. When I heard the historical part of it related, I at once said it was the writings of Solomon Spaulding. Soon after, I obtained the book, and on reading it, found much of it the same as Spaulding had written, more than twenty years before.

(Signed)
Oliver Smith[f]

---

[f]Howe, pp. 284-85.

This is in complete agreement with the eight witnesses in Conneaut who have already been quoted. Nahum Howard, for example, agreed that, concerning *The Book of Mormon*, he believed it to be "the same as Spalding wrote, except the religious part.[g] As the town physician, Howard would have had ample opportunity to converse with Spalding, who was continually in poor health.

In our first looks at Spalding and his writing, we presented the testimony of Henry Lake, Spalding's partner, and his conviction that *The Book of Mormon* was taken from Spalding's work. In 1880, Lake's son, Hiram, provided his own testimony concerning his father, Aaron Wright, John Miller, and Nathan Howard. He said:

> I am sixty-nine years of age, and have lived all my life in Conneaut, Ashtabula Co., Ohio. My father, Henry Lake, was partner with Solomon Spalding, in 1811 and 1812, in a forge in Conneaut (then Salem). About 1834, when I was about twenty-three years of age, I remember that there was a great excitement concerning Mormonism in Conneaut. My father read the "Book of Mormon," or heard it read, and was familiar with its contents, and he told me it was unquestionably derived from a manuscript written by his former partner, Solomon Spaulding, called "Manuscript Found; or, the Lost Tribes." I believe my father, about this time, made an affidavit to the same effect, which was published. Since 1834 I have conversed with Aaron Wright, John N. Miller, and Nathan Howard, old residents here, now deceased, all of whom lived here in 1811 and 1812, and who had heard Spaulding's manuscript read, and they told me they believed the "Book of Mormon" was derived from Spaulding's "Manuscript Found." Some or all

---

[g]Ibid., pp. 285-86.

these persons made affidavits to this effect, which were published in a book called "Mormonism Unveiled," edited by E. D. Howe, of Painesville, Ohio.
HIRAM LAKE[h]

Not only did Hiram confirm the testimonies of Lake, Wright, Miller, and Howard, but Lorin Gould confirmed Hiram's statement with his own statement on the same date (December 23, 1880, in Conneaut):

I have resided in the neighborhood of Conneaut, Ashtabula Co., Ohio, sixty-six years. During all that period I have known Hiram Lake, whose statement dated December 23d, 1880, I have read. This statement I believe to be true. I was acquainted with Henry Lake, Aaron Wright, John N. Miller, and Nathan Howard, the persons named in Hiram Lake's statement, and about 1834-35, the time of the excitement concerning Mormonism, I heard them all say that the "Book of Mormon" was undoubtedly taken from a manuscript written by Solomon Spaulding, which they had heard Spaulding read in 1811 or 1812, called "The Manuscript Found; or, the Lost Tribes."
(Signed)
Lorin Gould[i]

Rachel Derby was the daughter of John Miller and remembered most of her father's part in the controversy. She especially remembered his encounter with Hurlbut and his comments on hearing *The Book of Mormon* read.

My father, John N. Miller, settled in Springfield, Erie County, Pa., near Conneaut, Ohio, in 1800. He was elder of the Presbyterian Church over thirty years, and his father was before him. I have many times heard father say that in 1811 he and Andrew Cochran helped

---

[h]Dickinson, pp. 257-58.
[i]Ibid., p. 258.

build a forge or furnace for General Keyes at Conneaut, Ohio, and that they boarded with Solomon Spaulding, who had been a preacher, but his wife was not religious. She was high-strung, a frolicker, fond of balls and parties, and drove him out of the ministry. He said he liked Spaulding. While they were at their meals Spaulding would lie on the bed and read to them his manuscripts. Father also frequently read them himself. I have often heard him tell about the Nephites and Zerahemlites before the "Book of Mormon" was published. I well remember D. P. Hurlbut's coming to our house about fifty years ago, and his telling father that he was taking evidence to expose Mormonism, and hearing him read from the "Book of Mormon." Frequently father would request Hurlbut to stop reading and he would state what followed and Hurlbut would say that it was so in the "Book of Mormon." He expressed great surprise that father remembered so much of it. Father told him that the "Manuscript Found" was not near all of Spaulding's writings and that probably there would soon be another prophecy out. Father said he had no doubt the historical part of the "Book of Mormon" was Spaulding's "Manuscript Found." John Spaulding, Solomon's brother, lived half a mile from our house and our families were quite intimate. I saw father sign a statement and give Hurlbut. He had statements from Henry Lake, Aaron Wright and Dr. Howard, of Conneaut. Hurlbut stayed two nights with a Mormon woman of very bad character, who lived alone. Several of the lowest families in Springfield became Mormons. Mr. Hartshorn, a Mormon, whose wife was a Methodist, did not want to go West, but he insisted and she hung herself on the way.

(Signed)
Rachel Derby

Witnessed by:
Lee Derby, A. B. Deming.[j]

---

[j]Deming, p. 4 (Derby's statement given in Springfield, Pennsylvania, on December 9, 1884).

This information should be sufficient to show not only that the witnesses to the Spalding/Mormon connection were reliable, but also that their various testimonies agreed in all facts with each other. Far from indicating collusion, this shows that all the witnesses were well-acquainted with the facts, and, being persons of noble character, testified truthfully to what they knew. Mormon aspersions on the character of the witnesses fail to account for the mass of corroboration and the upright personal character of the persons who made the statements.

Appendix

A Review of
Dean Jessee's Critique

On August 20, 1977, after the news broke concerning our discovery of Spalding's handwriting in the original *Book of Mormon*, The Church of Jesus Christ of Latter Day Saints issued a press release and a report concerning our find. Its first paragraph read, "Conclusive evidence refuting charges by three California anti-Mormon researchers concerning the origin of the Book of Mormon has been released by a historian for The Church of Jesus Christ of Latter-day Saints."

After reading the evidence presented in this book, it might seem almost redundant for us to respond to the historian's report. However, we felt that a brief direct response to this report written by historian Dean C. Jessee was necessary. Due to space limitations and the fact that conclusive evidence has already been presented in the preceding pages of this book, our answers to the charges will be brief.

1. Jessee questions the character of D. P. Hurlbut, the man who collected the eight affidavits, in an attempt to nullify the affidavits themselves. However, it doesn't really matter who Hurlbut was. He never met Spalding and never saw (or heard read) *Manuscript Found*. We are not interested in *his* testimony, but only in the testimony of the eight witnesses. These eight witnesses *did* know Spalding and *Manuscript Found*, and it was *they* who approved of the statements and signed them. (Jessee's statement that Spalding's wife signed a statement gathered by Hurlbut is erroneous—it was *Martha* Spalding, Solomon's sister-in-law.) In addition, these eight witnesses each gave his *own* statement; all eight did not sign the *same* statement as did the eight witnesses to *The Book of Mormon*.

Jessee, in harmony with Fawn Brodie, disliked the consistency among the eight statements. If eight people bear consistent testimony in a court of law, the judge ordinarily concludes that their testimony is true. However, Jessee is not consistent in his own report. On page 2 he dismisses the eight witnesses because their statements "had such a suspicious similarity to them . . ." while on page 4 he dismisses Spalding's widow's testimony as well as his daughter's statement because "these and other statements on the subject contained so many inconsistencies. . . ." With that kind of logic, no affidavit in the world would satisfy Jessee!

Despite all the "suspicious similarities" in the eight testimonies, there are also minor differences (but no contradictions). For example, Henry Lake was the only one of the eight witnesses who remembered the contradiction in *Manuscript Found* which he told Spalding to change but which still appears today as a contradiction in *The Book of Mormon*. As was shown by Appendix 4, these eight witnesses were all upstanding citizens, and never retracted their statements. These people were alive when Howe's book was published and could easily have refuted its statements if they disagreed with them. Instead, these statements have stood firm throughout the years. In addition to these eight witnesses, Hurlbut collected many other testimonies from neighbors and friends of the Smiths, and again the testimony was consistent—Smith was a disreputable "glass-looker" (see Appendix 2). History is showing us today that those testimonies were accurate.

2. Jessee implies in his paper that the theory of two Spalding manuscripts was not devised until *Manuscript Story* (Spalding's first, unfinished novel) was found and the witnesses discovered that they were "wrong." This is not the case, since several of the witnesses had *already* signed statements designating more than one manuscript or novel (see Chapter 7, pages 154-160). The witnesses knew of *Manuscript Story* and some of Spalding's other works, but they also knew that this was *not* the manuscript they identified with *The Book of Mormon*. (For example, see Mrs. McKinstry's handwritten statement in Chapter 7, page 159). Jessee did not mention the fact that Howe (who bought Hurlbut's materials and wrote the book *Mormonism Unveiled*) was not trying to hide the existence of *Manuscript Story*. Instead, he even printed a summary of it in his book.

Jessee also stated that there is no similarity between *Manuscript Story* and *The Book of Mormon*. He says, "The document [*Manuscript Story*] bears no resemblance to the Book of Mormon that could not be found in many other books written in the same language. It is not written in the same style, nor are there common incidents or names. The Book of Mormon is highly religious in tone, the Spalding manuscript entirely secular."

This contention has nothing to do with our case, since it is not *Manuscript Story* that we are trying to identify with *The Book of Mormon*. We have repeatedly stated that *Manuscript Story* is not *The Book of Mormon*. We believe that *The Book of Mormon* is essentially Spalding's *second* novel.

However, as we show in Appendix 8, common authorship of the two documents is illustrated by the methods of literary criticism. Jessee's statement simply does not fit the facts.

3. One of the most glaring errors in Jessee's report concerns the testimony he attributes to Spalding's widow. Jessee's argument is that since Spalding's widow gave few details concerning her husband's novel in her first testimony to Hurlbut, and many details concerning it in her second testimony, she could be suspected of manufacturing those details. We have already pointed out that Jessee was confused. This was not Spalding's *widow's* testimony, but his *sister-in-law's* testimony! According to Spalding's daughter, she and her mother were highly suspicious of Hurlbut and were reluctant to give him *any* information about *any* of the details of Spalding's literary pursuits. The only reason Hurlbut was given permission to take the manuscript from Clark's home in New York was the plea of Mrs. Davison's brother, Sabine, who sent a letter with Hurlbut urging her to grant him permission. The details of her testimony given much later are not due to what Jessee calls a "rejuvenation of memory," but to her conviction that the facts

must be given to the public. She had a great deal more trust in the public than she ever had in Hurlbut. Even so, her testimony is not in great detail (see Chapter 3, pages 43-46).

4. Jessee's next contention appears to be based on some misconceptions by Mrs. Davison concerning the fate of *Manuscript Found*. According to him she cannot be trusted when testifying to the novel's identification with *The Book of Mormon*, but she *can* be trusted when testifying that the manuscript was returned by the printer to Spalding. As we have already explained in Chapter 3 and Appendix 3, Mrs. Davison was mistaken when she thought the manuscript was ultimately returned to her husband. In fact, Rigdon took the copy which was at Patterson's, and all that Spalding had was his own copy. This was both his own testimony and the testimony of all others who knew of the situation.

We need to remember that the important points in what Spalding's Amity acquaintances remembered are that the manuscript was stolen and that Rigdon's name was used *by Spalding* long before Mormonism or Rigdon became prominent. Spalding's friend Miller said that a *copy* of the manuscript was stolen and that Spalding himself told him that. The copy that would have been in the trunk would have been Spalding's personal copy. If *The Book of Mormon* could have an original manuscript and a printer's copy before its publication, couldn't the same be true of *Manuscript Found*?

5. Jessee next tackled the issue of the title appearing on *Manuscript Story*. Avoiding the issue of the title, *Manuscript Story*, which appears on the wrapper of the Oberlin manuscript, Jessee says:

Further indication that the double manuscript theory

is a forced interpretation is seen from the fact that the Spalding document at Oberlin contains no holograph title. Someone other than Spalding has written "Solomon Spaulding's Writings" in ink on a cover page, and then in light pencil over the top of this, the same hand has added "Manuscript Story" and "Conneaut Creek." There is nothing on the manuscript itself to suggest that Spalding ever wrote more than the one document, or that he was ever aware of the title "Manuscript Story," or that the document may not originally have been titled "Manuscript Found" and that someone removed it and supplied a title that would help perpetuate the theory.

The facts are that when L. L. Rice discovered the Spalding manuscript in 1884, he stated that he found it with a brown paper wrapper tied with a string. After he became aware of its contents he wrote, in ink, "Solomon's Spalding's Writings." Neither he nor Mr. Fairchild, who later obtained possession of the manuscript from Rice, wrote "Manuscript Story— Conneaut Creek"—according to their *own* statements! How can Jessee possibly say that the two lines were in the same hand? If Jessee is so terribly wrong in his identification of *this* handwriting, can we rely on his attempts to identify the handwriting of the Unidentified Scribe section of *The Book of Mormon*?

Spalding's daughter distinctly remembered the title *Manuscript Found* on the cover of her father's *second* novel. In a statement signed by her *after* she read *Manuscript Story*, she said it was *not* the same as *Manuscript Found*, which she had seen *many times*. She even said that she wondered if the Mormons thought they could deceive the public by calling *Manuscript Story—Conneaut Creek* by the title of *Manuscript Found* (see Chapter 7, pages 159-60)!

Since Rice admitted writing "Solomon Spalding's

Writings," but not the other line on the wrapper, we must conclude either that Rice was lying or that *someone else* wrote the line. Why would Rice lie? After all, at the time he believed that his find *disproved* the Spalding theory. He would hardly complicate the issue by erasing "Manuscript Found"—the type of proof he would have needed to prove his theory—and writing in "Manuscript Story."

Fairchild in later years did issue a statement saying that there could be two manuscripts after all. Both he and Rice had simply not been thoroughly acquainted with all the facts in their earlier years.

6. Jessee clouds the issue of how Smith obtained the manuscript by saying that the reports conflict—one saying that Rigdon stole it, and another saying that Smith stole it. For something to *conflict*, there must be no possible or reasonable way to reconcile the two accounts. This is certainly not the case here. The witnesses consistently declare that Rigdon stole the manuscript from Patterson's Print Shop in Pittsburgh, and that the fate of the second manuscript, in the widow's trunk, is unknown. Some have speculated that Smith *may* have taken it—but this would have been the *second* copy, not the first.

7. It would appear from Jessee's report that the only evidence we have that Rigdon actually knew Smith before he was supposed to have is the mention of a "mysterious stranger." As Chapter 6 so clearly showed, this is not the case. There is testimony on top of testimony placing Rigdon in Palmyra, and in close association with Smith, long before Mormonism began. Daniel Hendrix said that he spoke with Rigdon several times before 1830, and that Rigdon even had hopes of converting him to Mormonism!

8. Jessee's assertion that Rigdon never admitted his

guilty. He did tell J. Jeffries privately in 1844 that he had taken Spalding's manuscript, although for obvious reasons Rigdon declined to repeat this admission publicly.

A careful study of the function of the Danites in Mormonism gives us another reason for understanding Rigdon's reluctance to come forward with the truth even after he left the Mormon Church. According to careful research, it has been determined that the Danites existed to punish and murder those people (Mormon and non-Mormon) who were injurious to the fledging church. Rigdon himself said, according to Mrs. Nancy Alexander (who lived next to the Smith family and who knew Rigdon very well) that he knew of the Danite activities. She said, "I heard Sidney Rigdon lecture in Kirtland after he left the Mormons. He said many Mormons who knew their secrets and left them were followed and murdered . . ." (given in Mentor, Ohio, and now in the possession of the Chicago Historical Society).

9. Jessee's attempt to argue the issue of handwriting need only be weighed against the testimony found in Chapter 7 of this book.

10. The eight witnesses' declaration that *Manuscript Found* was *The Book of Mormon* "except for the religious matter" does not preclude numerous references to religion in *Manuscript Found*, since *some* changes in religious matters were undoubtedly made to Spalding's manuscript after it was taken from Patterson's Print Shop.

11. Most of the rest of Jessee's dissertation concerns itself with identifying the handwriting. We do not accept Jessee's credentials. We know of no judge or court in the United States of America that would accept his creden-

tials as far as handwriting identification is concerned. He is not a court-qualified Examiner of Questioned Documents. He has never been formally trained in this highly technical and scientific art, which takes many years of specialized study. (See Appendix 6 for typical credentials.)

There are other amateurs who have tried their hands at identifying this handwriting who are no better qualified than Jessee. Both Jessee and these other self-styled experts are not experts at all, and their opinions are just that—opinions. They are worth nothing in a court of law.

For example, when the Joseph Smith Papyri were discovered (see Appendix 1), Mormon Egyptologist Dee Jay Nelson identified and translated the documents accurately as related to the Egyptian Book of the Dead, showing Smith's translations to be incorrect.

What was the Mormon Church's response? They simply ignored Nelson and assigned the job to a novice—one unqualified in the field, Hugh Nibley, in order to obtain a decision in their favor.

12. Jessee attempts to point out spelling errors in the twelve pages that are consistent with the errors in another document, dated 1831, which he claims is in the same handwriting. What he neglects to do is to show that the same types of errors also exist in what everyone, Mormon and non-Mormon alike, accepts as Spalding's literature, *Manuscript Story*! For example, Spalding often spells "dwell" without the final "l," as "dwel." The twelve pages and the 1831 document spell "shall" as "shal," again dropping the final l.

Both *Manuscript Found* and the "unidentified" section of *The Book of Mormon* use small letters when capitals should be used. Both substitute letters like "i" for "y," etc. If Kaye could find similarities among 2500 letter "t's," then we need not take Jessee's small study seriously. Handwriting examination should be left to the experts.

13. Although Jessee is right in stating that the style in *Manuscript Story* is different from that in *The Book of Mormon*, he does not mention, as we have, that the witnesses (not removed from the scene by 147 years, as Jessee is) declared that Spalding *altered* his first plan (*Manuscript Story*), and changed his style (*Manuscript Found*). In summary, Jessee could not have known everything we have uncovered in our years of research. How could he attempt to refute the overwhelming evidence presented in our book before it was even published? Even if there were no evidence that the handwriting in *The Book of Mormon* was that of Spalding, our thesis would still be proved from the abundant amount of evidence presented in the first six chapters of this book and in its appendixes. Spalding once remarked jokingly that in one hundred years time everyone would believe his book to be history except the learned men!

Appendix

Qualifications of Handwriting Experts

Each of the three document experts we hired to examine the questioned and known handwritings is well-known in his field and has had many years of experience in examining handwriting. Of the three men, Henry Silver was the oldest and had been in the field longer than either of the other two experts. He was the first expert we hired and the first to render his opinion on the documents. Due to ill health, Silver resigned the case before he examined all of the original documents, but his notarized statement based on the photocopies (which were certified as authentic by both the Mormon Church and the Ohio Library) supported our thesis that Spalding was the author of the "unidentified scribe" section of the original *Book of Mormon*. With this positive statement, we felt confident in hiring two other experts and in having them also furnish us with their statements.

We hired another expert, Howard Doulder. Doulder spent many years in the Questioned Document section of the Milwaukee Police Department before he joined the U.S. Treasury Department in 1955. Eighteen years later, in 1973, he retired from that department and entered private practice.

William Kaye's career began in 1935, and since that time his clientele has included government agencies, banks, insurance companies, railroads, finance companies, stores, and manufacturers. He is especially expert at identifying signatures and handwriting on questioned wills. After Kaye had given us his statement on the photocopies (he did not know of Henry Silver's involvement or conclusion, nor did he know what verdict we were hoping for, nor did he know that the documents had anything to do with Mormonism), we were sure that our thesis was correct, and that Kaye and Silver, with the reputation each had, were reliable supporters of our claim.

Before we had hired any of these three experts, we had asked for their credentials and experience. For the interested reader, we have here reproduced those credentials as they were given to us.

Qualified Handwriting Expert
Examiner of Questioned Documents

Henry Silver had eight years formal training in handwriting identification, including the physiological and psychological factors in handwriting, and during the same time he had training in the identification of typewriting, ink, and paperstock — four years training at The

Independent Institute, Sydney, Australia, from 1914 to 1918, and four years under direction of David Huegan, from 1921 to 1925, internationally known handwriting expert and examiner of questioned documents who practiced in Vienna and Paris.

Mr. Silver has practiced professionally in Los Angeles for more than forty years. He has given several thousand reports on questioned handwriting and documents to attorneys, doctors, banks, insurance and finance companies, industrial and other business concerns. The list includes such names as Security First National, California, Crocker, Union, and Farmers and Merchants banks; Peoples' Finance and Ark Finance Companies of Beverly Hills; Allstate, Farmers, and State Farm Insurance Companies; Firestone and Uniroyal Rubber Companies; Manpower Inc. and Budget Inc.; Howard Hughes Nevada Operations; etc., etc.

Mr. Silver has testified several hundred times in civil and criminal cases on questioned handwriting or documents, including federal, superior, and municipal courts in Los Angeles and in many other California cities, as well as in Alaska, Arizona, Nevada, Nebraska, South Carolina, Texas, and Louisiana.

Mr. Silver has been engaged to lecture on identification subjects before law enforcement organizations, three times at Los Angeles City Hall before annual meetings of the legal secretaries of the administrative offices; Beverly Hills, Compton, International Airborne, and Bay Area Legal Secretaries Associations, with the latter sponsored by The Bay Area Bar Association; before California Bank employees, before California and L.A. Junior Chamber of Commerce Breakfast Clubs, Jonathan and Lions' Clubs, Masonic Lodges, Bank Officials' Exchange Club of Santa Monica, and three times at the

Hughes Tool and Aircraft Corporations. He has also been engaged to lecture twice before a branch of the Los Angeles County Medical Association, Women's Medical Association, Beverly Hills Dental Academy at Beverly Hills Hotel, So. Calif. Chiropractic Association, and before the annual convention at Las Vegas of medical doctors and dentists of the American Institute of Hypnosis. He has been engaged to lecture many times over radio and television broadcasts, and while on an around-the-world lecture tour from 1927 to 1929 was engaged to give a series of lectures on the subject over the government-controlled Radio Stations in Sydney, Australia, and BBC, London, England.

Mr. Silver has had several books published on the subject: two by The Independent Inst., Sydney, Aus., 1928; two by W. Foulsham & Co., London, 1928; one by Frye & Smith, San Diego, 1932; one by G. P. Putnam's Sons, New York City, 1929, which were placed in the public libraries throughout the United States in 1929.

HOWARD C. DOULDER
EXAMINER OF
QUESTIONED DOCUMENTS

Q. WHAT IS YOUR OCCUPATION OR PROFESSION?

A. Examiner of Questioned Documents, more commonly known as a handwriting expert.

Q. FOR WHOM AND WHERE ARE YOU EMPLOYED?

A. I am now in private practice. I was formerly employed as an examiner of questioned documents, Supervisor of the Alcohol, Tobacco and Firearms Crime Laboratory, United States Treasury Department, Chicago, Illinois.

Q. HOW LONG DID YOU HAVE THIS POSITION WITH THE TREASURY DEPT.?

A. From November 1955 to when I retired, June 30, 1973.

Q. WHAT POSITIONS, IF ANY, DID YOU HOLD BEFORE BEING EMPLOYED BY THE TREASURY DEPT.?

A. I was Assistant Document Examiner for the Milwaukee Police Department from June 1953 to November 1955. Prior to that I worked in the Identification Bureau of the Milwaukee Police Department on Photography, Fingerprints and Questioned Documents. I joined the Milwaukee Police Department in March 1947 and served as a Patrolman, Identification Technician and Assistant Document Examiner.

Q. WHAT PREPARATION HAVE YOU HAD TO PREPARE YOURSELF AS AN EXAMINER OF QUESTIONED DOCUMENTS?

A. My Preparation was by apprenticeship, under other experts of many years of experience, who taught and supervised me in the course of my training. I have also made a study of natural, disguised, simulated and traced handwriting and handprinting. I have studied numerous books on the subject and have kept abreast with the latest scientific developments in this field. I have also interchanged methods and ideas with many other experts in this field.

Q. WHAT WERE YOUR DUTIES WITH THE TREASURY DEPT.?

A. I was the Supervisor of the Laboratory and did scientific work which consisted of questioned Documents, fingerprints and photography for all divisions of the Treasury Department in a 38-state area.

Q. ARE YOU A MEMBER OF ANY TECHNICAL SOCIETY IN THE FIELD OF QUESTIONED DOCUMENTS?

A. Yes, I am a Fellow in the American Academy of Forensic Sciences and past Chairman of the Questioned Document Section. Also a member of the International Association for Identification, and twice past Chairman of the Questioned Document Section.

Q. HAVE YOU HAD OCCASIONS TO TESTIFY IN COURT PREVIOUS TO THIS DATE?

A. Yes, I have qualified and testified as a Document Examiner in Federal, State, Military and Tax Courts in most of the thirty-eight states that I serviced.

Q. APPROXIMATELY HOW MANY TIMES HAVE YOU QUALIFIED AND TESTIFIED IN COURT?

A. Approximately 400 times.

BACKGROUND AND QUALIFICATIONS

Born in Milwaukee, Wisconsin, June, 1923.

1947 to 1955—Milwaukee Police Department

Clerk Stenographer, Identification Technician, Patrolman and Assistant Document Examiner.

As a Clerk Stenographer took dictation at 125 words per minute.

As an identification technician processed prisoners, fingerprinting, photographing and obtaining personnel history. Taking, classifying and searching latent and ink fingerprints.

Obtaining known specimen handwriting. Participated in crime scene search for evidence, murders, robberies, rapes, etc. The taking, processing and printing of photographs.

As a patrolman did regular patrol duties and investigations.

As Assistant Document Examiner to Mr. Orville B. Livingston, who taught and supervised my study of natural, disguised, simulated and traced handwriting and handprinting.

Classifying handwriting and checks. Processed papers, checks, notes, etc. for latent fingerprints.

Examination and comparison of questioned documents and typewriting problems.

Studied numerous books on the subject and kept abreast with the latest scientific developments in these fields, interchanging methods and ideas with many other experts in these fields.

Qualified and testified in District courts.

Nov. 1955 to June 30, 1973 (retired)

Supervisor, Crime Laboratory, United States Treasury Dept., Chicago, Ill.

Assisted all enforcement agencies of the Treasury Department in a thirty-eight state area in the fields of questioned documents, fingerprints and specialized photography.

Also assisted cities, sheriffs, and attorney generals in numerous states in these fields of scientific investigations.

Lectured before the first Secret Service Questioned Document School, Washington D.C., in 1958.

Participated in scientific investigations of numerous police departments throughout the country.

Lectured and conducted numerous mock trials in regard to expert testimony on fingerprints and questioned documents at DePaul University, Chicago, Illinois.

During the years 1969, '70 and '71 conducted a three-hour credit course, "Scientific Criminal investigations," at St. Joseph's College, East Chicago, Indiana.

In 1968 assisted the U.S. Senate Sub-committee on Government Operations investigating riots, civil and criminal disorders. Testified before this senate subcommittee regarding the Chicago Blackstone Rangers fraud.

June 30th, 1973, to date.

Private practice in Chicago, Illinois, for two years.

Private practice in Honolulu, Hawaii, one year, and since November 1976 private practice in Orange County, California.

Am still retained as a consultant for the Board of Election Commissioners, Chicago, Illinois.

Member of the International Association for Identification since 1948 and twice Chairman of the Questioned Document Section.

I have qualified and testified approximately 300 times as an Examiner of Questioned Documents and Fingerprint Expert in federal, state, military and tax Courts in most of the thirty-eight States that I serviced, including Hawaii.

QUALIFICATION QUESTIONS
WILLIAM KAYE

1. WHAT IS YOUR OCCUPATION?

Examiner of questioned documents, commonly known as a handwriting expert.

2. WHEN AND HOW DID YOU START THIS WORK?

Through research at Emory University, Atlanta, Georgia. Later I studied under Robert E. Moore, Examiner of Questioned Documents for the Sheriff's Department, City of Detroit. I also was permitted to examine questioned documents in the offices of Albert S. Osborne.

3. WHAT WAS YOUR TRAINING?

I have a reference library of books on the subject which I have studied. In practical experience, I have examined thousands of cases with many types of document problems and I taught handwriting at Ferndale High School, Ferndale, Michigan.

4. CAN YOU EXAMINE HANDWRITING OF UNKNOWN ORIGIN AND COMPARE IT WITH HANDWRITING OF KNOWN ORIGIN, AND DETERMINE IF BOTH WERE WRITTEN BY THE SAME PERSON?

Yes.

5. DO YOU HAVE A LABORATORY IN CONNECTION WITH YOUR OFFICE?

Yes.

6. WHAT DOES YOUR LABORATORY AND OFFICE EQUIPMENT CONSIST OF?

Photographic equipment, microscopes, hand magnifiers, chemical reagents, measuring instruments, ultraviolet and infrared equipment.

7. WHAT SUBJECTS IN PARTICULAR HAVE YOU STUDIED IN ORDER TO QUALIFY YOURSELF IN THIS WORK?

I have studied handwriting and typewriting

identification, inks, paper, water marks, recovery of eradicated writing, the sequence of two lines, photography and chemistry.

8. OVER WHAT PERIOD HAS YOUR WORK EX-TENDED?

Established 1935

9. BEFORE WHAT COURTS HAVE YOU QUALI-FIED AS A WITNESS TO GIVE TESTIMONY AS A DOCUMENT EXAMINER?

In municipal, county and United States courts.
In the Surrogate Court and the Supreme Court of Canada.
Also, before grand juries, commissions and committees.
Appearances in all courts.

REPRESENTATIVE CLIENTS OF MR. KAYE

State Bar of Michigan
The courts, as consultant
Michigan Attorney General
National Labor Relations Board

BANKS

The National Bank of Detroit
The Detroit Bank & Trust Co.
The Michigan Bank
The Bank of the Commonwealth
The City Bank
The Public Bank
The Manufacturer's National Bank
Crocker Citizens Bank

Commonwealth Bank
Bank of America
Independence Bank
Home Savings & Loan

BONDING & INSURANCE COMPANIES

A.A.A.
Allstate Insurance Co.
Metropolitan Life Insurance Co.
Standard Accident Co.
Lawyers Title & Insurance Co.
State Farm Insurance Co.
Royal Globe Insurance Co.
U.S.F. & G.
Maccabbee's

FINANCE COMPANIES

Associates Discount Co.
Beneficial Finance Co.
Commercial Credit Co.
Household Finance Co.
Seaboard Finance Co.

MANUFACTURERS

Buick Motors Division
Cadillac Motors Division
Chevrolet Motors Division
Oldsmobile Motors Division
Chrysler Corporation
Firestone Tire & Rubber Co.
Sun Oil Company
Ford Motor Car Co.

RAILROADS

C. & O. Railway
Canadian National R. R.
Grand Trunk & Western R. R.
New York Central R. R.

STORES

The J. L. Hudson Co.
F. W. Woolworth Co.
Lane Bryant, Inc.
Montgomery Ward
Sears, Roebuck & Co.

MISCELLANEOUS

AFL-CIO
American Express Co.
Burton Abstract Co.
Holiday Inns
Hiram Walker & Co.
Michigan Federation of Teachers
Detroit Federation of Teachers
The Detroit News
The Detroit Free Press
Wayne State University

LIST OF DOCUMENT BOOKS
POSSESSED BY MR. KAYE

The following are some of the questioned document books in my library:

A. *Questioned Documents*, by Albert S. Osborne, 1929 edition.

B. *Photographic Evidence*, by Charles Scott, three

volumes. Mr. Scott is also an attorney and member of the Missouri Bar.

C. *Suspect Documents*, by Wilson R. Harrison.

D. *Law of Disputed Documents*, by J. Newton Baker.

E. *Disputed Documents*, by Hanna F. Sulner, 1966.

F. *Forgeries*, by George H. Zinnel.

G. *Typewriting Identification*, by Billy Prior Bates, and *Questioned Typewriting*.

H. *Problems of Proof*, by Columbia University Press Library.

I. *Modern Scientific Evidence*, by Richardson.

J. *Forensic Physics by Ultra-Violet Light: Preliminary Identification of Obliterated Writings in Forgeries and Falsification of Documents*, Cincinnatti.

K. *The W. H. Anferson Co.*, by James R. Richardson of the Kentucky Bar.

L. *Jones on Evidence—Civil and Criminal*. Spencer A. Gard.

M. *Basic Problems of Evidence*, By Edmund M. Morgan.

Professional & Personal References furnished upon request.

Appendix

Chronology Concerning the Fate of Solomon Spalding's Copy of Manuscript Found

1816, October 20	Solomon Spalding died in Amity, Pennsylvania.
1816 (or 17)-1820	Mrs. Spalding and her daughter moved (with the manuscript in a trunk) to live with her brother, William Sabine, in Onandoga Valley, New York. Mrs. Spalding's daughter read the manuscript often, as did the entire family, as well as friends, acquaintances, and boarders.
1820-30	Mrs. Spalding married Mr. Davison, and they (including the daughter) moved to Hartwick, New York, where the daughter again frequently read the manuscript until some time before her marriage in 1828.

1823-27	In her later years, Mrs. Davison (Spalding) stated that during this time there was a young man constantly loitering around their house whose name was Smith. She states that he was arrested several times for it.
1826	Joseph Smith was arrested, tried, and convicted of fortune-telling in Bainbridge, New York, only thirty miles from Hartwick, where the Davisons were living.
1828	Daughter married Mr. McKinstry and moved to Munson, Massachusetts. There is no testimony that anyone saw the manuscript after this date (probably the daughter had not seen it for a year or two).
1830	Mrs. (Spalding) Davison left Mr. Davison and went to live with her cousin, Jerome Clark, still in the town of Hartwick. She moved the trunk with her, and, without looking, assumed that the manuscript was still in it.
1831-44	Mrs. (Spalding) Davison moved to Munson, Massachusetts, to live with her daughter and son-in-law. She left the trunk with her cousin, Jerome Clark, in Hartwick. She died in 1844.
1834	Mr. Hurlbut, sent by the community of Conneaut, Ohio, to verify that *The Book of Mormon* was Spalding's second novel, opened the trunk and could find no manuscript.

Appendix

Parallels Between Manuscript Story and The Book of Mormon

The edition of *Manuscript Story* published by the Mormon Church states concerning the comparison between *The Book of Mormon* and *Manuscript Story*, ". . . there is not one sentence, one incident, or one proper name common to both, and . . . the oft boasted similarity in matter and nomenclature is utterly false."[a] Similarly, Mormon David Whitmer declared: "There is no similarity whatever between it [*Manuscript Story*] and *The Book of Mormon*."[b]

We began our own examination of the two books, and we found scores of similarities. This careful comparison convinced Cowdrey that the Mormon Church had lied to him. Cowdrey requested that his name be

---

[a]*Manuscript Story*, Deseret Publishers, preface to the 1886 edition.
[b]Whitmer, *An Address to All Believers in Christ*, p. 11.

taken off the membership rolls of the Church of Jesus Christ of Latter Day Saints, stating that he was convinced that Solomon Spalding was the true source of *The Book of Mormon.* However, according to the Mormon hierarchy, no one can ever resign from the Mormon Church. A person can only be "excommunicated by his own request." This is what happened to Cowdrey. (Later he became an evangelical Christian). During his trial, he brought forth some of the many parallels between the two books, some reproduced here. According to Cowdrey, Bishop Stuart Waldrip was unable to present a satisfactory defense in the face of the many obvious similarities.

Often common authorship can be seen by literary and linguistic clues as well as by handwriting and other testimony. Literary or higher criticism is a technique which includes vocabulary analysis, event analysis, spelling idiosyncrasies, and other literary characteristics.

In this appendix, we are investigating common authorship of both *The Book of Mormon* and *Manuscript Story*, Spalding's first novel. Since the evidence already presented shows Spalding as the originator of *The Book of Mormon*, first known as *Manuscript Found*, the literary critic should be able to find evidence of that common authorship through linguistic traits and characteristics common to both works.

We have found these parallels between Spalding's first novel and his second (revised by others but essentially the same as he first wrote). We present here some of the parallels and spelling traits illuminating the conclusion that Spalding was the author of both manuscripts. We are not saying that the parallels are identical to each other. We are saying that the similarities between the two sets of parallels are to be expected, since

Spalding was the author of the two novels which both deal with the same basic subject matter.

Discovery of the Manuscript

Manuscript Story: Near the west bank of the Conneaut river there are the remains of an ancient fort. As I was walking. . . . I happened to tread on a flat stone. This was a small distance from the fort and it lay on the top of a great small mound of earth exactly horizontal. The face of it had a singular appearance. . . . I found a earthen box with a cofer which shut perfectly tight. . . . My mind filled with awful sensations which . . . would hardly permit my hands to remove this venerable deposit.

. . . The box was taken and raised to open it. . . . With the assistance of a lever I raised the stone. But you may easily conjecture my astonishment when I discovered that its ends and sides rested on stones and that it was designed as a cover to an artificial cave. . . . When I had removed the cover I found that it contained 18 rolls of parchment.

J. Smith's History: Convenient to the village of Manchester, Ontario county, New York, stands a hill of considerable size, and the most elevated of any in the neighborhood. On the west of this hill, not far from the top, under a stone of considerable size, lay the plates, deposited in a stone box. This stone was thick and rounding in the middle on the upper side, and thinner towards the edges, so that the middle part of it was visible above the ground, but the edge all around was covered with earth. Having removed the earth, I obtained a lever, which I got fixed under the edge of the stone, and . . . raised it up. I looked in, and there indeed did I behold the plates. . . . The box was formed by laying stones together.

Seer Stones

Manuscript Story: A seer by the name of Hamack holds "in his hand . . . a stone which he pronounced transparent, through this . . . he could behold . . . dark intrigues. . . . Hamack . . . could view things present and things to come. Could behold the dark intrigues and cabals of foreign courts. . . . He could behold the galant and his mistress in their bedchamber. . . . [Hamack would also look] firmly and steadfastly on the stone and raised his prophetic voice . . . discover hidden treasure, secluded from the eyes of other mortals . . . such was the clearness of his sight, when this transparent stone was placed before his eyes. . . ."

Book of Mormon: . . . and the Lord said, "I will prepare unto my servant Gazelem, a stone, which shall shine forth in darkness unto light, that I may discover unto my people who serve me . . . did molten out of a rock sixteen small stones and they were white and clear, even as transparent glass.". . . [certain stones were] called interpreters and no man can look in them except he is commanded, lest he should look for that he ought not and whosoever is commanded to look in them, the same is called seer. . . . A seer can know of things which are past, and also of things which are to come, and by them shall all things be revealed, or, rather shall secret things be made manifest. . . . Whoso shall hide up treasures in the earth shall find them again no more . . . save he be a righteous man.

The Solar System

Manuscript Story: This scheme [the operation of the universe] will represent the solar system as displaying the transcendant wisdom of its Almighty architect for in this we behold the sun suspended by Omnipotence and all the planets around him as their common center in exact order and harmony.

Book of Mormon: All things denote there is a God; yea even the earth, and all things that are upon the face of it, yea, and its motion, yea, and also all the planets which move in their regular form do witness that there is a Supreme Creator.

Community Property

Manuscript Story: Our community might be said to be one family . . . the property was common stock. What was produced by our labor was likewise to be common. All subject to the distribution of the judges.

Book of Mormon: And they had all things common among them, every man dealing justly, one with another.

Description of Forts

Manuscript Story: On page 74, ". . . the walls were formed of dirt which was taken in front of the fort. . . ." In addition to this they inserted pieces of timber on top of the ramparts. "These pieces were about seven ft. in length from the ground to the top. . . . A deep canal or trench would likewise be formed."

Book of Mormon: [They threw up] heaps of earth round about all the cities . . . and upon the top of these ridges of earth he caused that there should be timbers . . . works of timbers built up to the height of a man . . . a frame of pickets built upon the timbers round about . . . a ditch which had been dug round about.

Discovery of Manuscripts

Solomon Spalding: In a letter of January 6,

1855, at Eastford, Connecticut, Josiah Spalding stated: "My brother told me that a young man told him that he had a wonderful dream. He dreamed that he himself opened a great mound, where there were human bones. There he found a written history that would answer the inquiry respecting the civilized people that once inhabitated that country until they were destroyed by the savages.

Joseph Smith: From Joseph Smith's History (2:34, 42): "While he [Moroni] was conversing with me about the plates, the vision was opened to my mind that I could see the place where the plates were deposited, . . . giving an account of the former inhabitants of this continent."

Literary Trait Comparisons

Many people consistently repeat certain types of literary peculiarities, and the literary critic is interested in those types of peculiarities which are somewhat uncommon and thus distinguish a particular author. An examination of some of the peculiarities in *Manuscript Story* and *The Book of Mormon* shows that both pieces could easily have originated with the same author.

For example, *Manuscript Story* often denotes the past tense of verbs which end in "y" by changing the "y" to "i" and adding "ed." Thus, *employed* becomes, in *Manuscript Story, emploid*. This idiosyncrasy is repeated often in *The Book of Mormon* in exactly the same way.

Both *Manuscript Story* and *The Book of Mormon* often use the letter *t* where an *ed* is correct (example: *lookt* for *looked, claspt* for *clasped*). Spalding was inconsistent regarding double consonants. We find in both *Manuscript Story* and *The Book of Mormon* (derived from Spalding's second novel, *Manuscript Found*), that Spalding often omitted double consonants in the same words that he sometimes spelled correctly. (For example, *vilage* was used for *village*, yet sometimes the word would be correct in the manuscript as *village*.) His peculiar treatment of double consonants was especially evident in words ending with double consonants, in which case he almost invariably, in both works, dropped one of the double consonants (*Manuscript Story*: *dwel*; *Book of Mormon*: *shal*).

Both novels of Spalding (*Book of Mormon*, which used to be *Manuscript Found*, and *Manuscript Story*, his first novel) contain dozens of words with letters transposed. *Treu* appears instead of *true*, *exampel* instead of *example*, and other transpositions paralleling each other throughout both works. In many places Spalding spelled words phonetically rather than correctly. In both *The Book of Mormon* and *Manuscript Story* this trait is evident in such words as *hart* for *heart*, *thot* for *thought*, and *sot* for *sought*.

Finally, one of the grammar problems both in *The Book of Mormon* and *Manuscript Story* is that of running sentences together in the manuscripts. Spalding, as the author of the two works, would not normally be expected to commit mistakes as obvious as run-on sentences, since he was a graduate of Dartmouth College. However, both *Manuscript Story* and *The Book of Mormon* claimed to have been translations of lost histories of the American Indians, and Spalding wanted to lend as much credibility as possible to his historical novel. He apparently hoped to do this by allowing sentences to run together, thus appearing to be freshly translated without editor's punctuations. Both *Manuscript Story* and *The Book of Mormon* contain many examples of this literary device.

The preceding examples of parallels between Spalding's two novels are not surprising, because of the novels' common authorship and because both novels were on the same topic. We have presented only a few of the many parallels that exist between the two works. While literary criticism by itself cannot prove common authorship, it can point out common authorship traits. The Mormon Church has repeatedly said that there was not one thing in common between the two works. The church even went so far as to say that *Manuscript Story*, unlike *The Book of Mormon*, was entirely secular. We have investigated those charges carefully, and the results of our thorough study have included numerous parallels and appearances of religious matter in *Manuscript Story*. The Mormon claims are simply incorrect. Anyone who objectively investigates the parallels between Spalding's two works can readily reach the same conclusion we have. In this brief appendix we have listed only a few of the parallels we found, but a forthcoming book will fully detail the similarities. Our examination of the two manuscripts has led us to completely reject the claims of the Mormon Church that the two have nothing in common.

Bibliography

1. Adair, James, *The History of the American Indians*. New York: Promontory Press, 1930 (originally published in London in 1775).

2. *American Review*, "Yankee Mahomet," New York, June 1851.

3. Bennett, John C., *The History of the Saints; or an Expose of Joe Smith and Mormonism*. Boston: Leland & Whiting, 1842.

4. Bodine, Jerry and Marian, *Witnessing to the Mormon*. San Juan Capistrano, CA: Christian Research Institute, 1977.

5. *The Book of Mormon*. Salt Lake City: Deseret News Press, 1971.

6. Brodie, Fawn M., *No Man Knows My History*. New York: Alfred Knopf, 1971.

7. Cheesman, Paul R., *The Keystone of Mormonism*. Salt Lake City: Deseret Books, 1973.

8. Clark, John Alonzo, *Gleanings by the Way*. Philadelphia: W.J. & J.K. Simon, 1842.

9. Deming, Arthur B., *Naked Truths About Mormonism*. Oakland, CA: self-published periodical, 1888.

10. *Deseret Evening News*, "Original Manuscript of the Book of Mormon." Salt Lake City, 1899.

11. Dickinson, Ellen E., *New Light on Mormonism*. New York: Funk & Wagnalls, 1885.

12. Dodd, W. L., *The Early History of Amity, Pennsylvania*. Privately published in Pennsylvania, 1940.

13. Gregg, Thomas, *The Prophet of Palmyra*. New York: J.B. Alden, 1890.

14. Howard, Richard D., *Restoration Scripture*. Independence, MO: Herald Publishing House, 1969.

15. Howe, Eber D., *Mormonism Unveiled*. Painesville, OH: published by the author, 1834 (also as *History of the Mormons* in 1840).

16. Jessee, Dean C., *Brigham Young University Studies*, "The Original Book of Mormon Manuscript," vol. 10, Spring 1970, pp. 259-78.

17. Kelly, L. E., and Braden, Clark, *Public Discussion of the Issues Between the Reorganized Church of Jesus Christ of Latter Day Saints—and Church of Christ (Disciples)*. Lamoni, IA: Reorganized Church Publishing, 1913.

18. Linn, William A., *The Story of the Mormons*. New York: The MacMillan Co., 1902.

19. Martin, Walter R., *Kingdom of the Cults*. Minneapolis: Bethany Fellowship, 1965.

20. McFarland, Joseph F., *20th Century History of the City of Washington and Washington County, Pennsylvania*. Chicago: Richmond-Arnold, 1910.

21. Nibley, Preston, *The Witnesses of the Book of Mormon*. Salt Lake City: Deseret News Press, 1953.

22. Page, John E., *The Spaulding Story*. Plano, IL: Reorganized Church of Latter Day Saints, 1866.

23. Patterson, Robert, Jr., *History of Washington County, Pennsylvania, with Biographical Sketches of Many of Its Pioneers and Prominent Men*, "Who Wrote the Book of Mormon." Philadelphia: Everts & Co., 1882.

24. *Pittsburgh Gazette*, Pittsburgh, PA, 1812-16.

25. *Pittsburgh Mercury*, Pittsburgh, PA, 1812-17.

26. *Pittsburgh Telegraph*, Pittsburgh, PA, February 6, 1879.

27. *Scribner's Monthly*, "The Book of Mormon," August 1880.

28. Smith, Lucy, *Biographical Sketches of Joseph Smith the Prophet and His progenitors for Many Generations*. Liverpool: S.W. Richards, 1853.

29. Shook, Charles, *The True Origin of the Book of Mormon*. Cincinnatti: The Standard Publishing Co., 1914.

30. Spaulding, Charles Warren, *The Spaulding Memorial: A Genealogical History of Edward Spaulding and His Descendants*. Chicago, 1897.

31. Spaulding, Solomon, *The Manuscript Found or the Manuscript Story*. Lamoni, IA: Reorganized LDS, 1885.

32. Spaulding, Rev. Solomon, *The Manuscript Story*. Salt Lake City: Deseret Books, 1886.

33. *The Washington Reporter*, Wed., April 21, 1860.

34. Whitmer, David, *An Address to All Believers in Christ*. Richmond, MO: published by the author, 1887.

35. Williams, Samuel, *Mormonism Exposed*. Pittsburgh: published by the author, 1842.

36. Winchester, Benjamin, *The Origin of the Spaulding Story*. Philadelphia, 1840.

37. Wyl, W., *Mormon Portraits or the Truth About the Mormon Leaders—From 1830-1886*. Salt Lake City: The Salt Lake City Tribune Printing & Publishing Co., 1886.